SINGAPORE
1819

A LIVING LEGACY

SINGAPORE 1819

A LIVING LEGACY

KENNIE TING

TALISMAN

First published in 2019
First Paperback edition in 2019

Talisman Publishing Pte Ltd
52 Genting Lane #06-05
Ruby Land Complex 1
Singapore 349560
talisman@apdsing.com
www.talismanpublishing.com

ISBN 978-981-14-0816-8

Editor Kim Inglis
Copy Editor Paul Haines
Design Norreha Sayuti, Stephy Chee
Studio Manager Janice Ng
Publisher Ian Pringle

PAGE 2: View of the Singapore
River today, with the Fullerton
Hotel and the global financial
centre at Raffles Place.

CONTENTS

Singapore — Port City

"MY DEAR SIR, – Here I am at Singapore, true to my word, and in the enjoyment of all the pleasure which a footing on such classic ground must inspire. The lines of the old city, and of its defences, are still to be traced, and within its ramparts the British Union waves unmolested [...] Most certainly the Dutch never had a factory in the island of Singapore; and it does not appear to me that their recent arrangements with a subordinate authority at Rhio can or ought to interfere with our permanent establishment here. [...] This place possesses an excellent harbour, and everything that can be desired for a British port in the island of St John's, which forms the south-western point of the harbour. We have commanded an intercourse with all ships passing through the Straits of Singapore. We are within a week's sail of China, close to Siam, and in the very seat of the Malayan Empire. [...] If I keep Singapore I shall be quite satisfied; and in a few years our influence over the Archipelago, as far as concerns our commerce, will be fully established."

— Letter from Sir Thomas Stamford Raffles to
William Marsden, Singapore, 31st January 1819

A visitor standing on the banks of the Singapore River, a bit to the north of the Asian Civilisations Museum where a white statue of Sir Thomas Stamford Raffles stands today, would be forgiven for thinking he or she was gazing at a mirage across the river at Boat Quay; so starkly and impossibly rise the skyscrapers of the World Financial District, jostling with each other like towering trees competing for sunlight in a tropical rainforest. At the foot of these skyscrapers, dwarfed but not overwhelmed, stand a tidy row of two-to-three storey former godowns or warehouses, once housing spices, resins and raw materials from all across Asia and the Malay Archipelago, today home to restaurants, bars and the offices of architecture, design and advertising firms.

Two hundred years ago, the view would have been different.

Then, the island was a sleepy fishing village at the periphery of global trade. The "Singapore" of the time — the grand emporium and entrepôt port of the East — was the Dutch city of Batavia (today's Jakarta), sitting at the northwesterly end of the island of Java. The Dutch were the unchallenged masters of the Eastern Seas, controlling two strategic Straits

OPPOSITE: View of the Singapore Waterfront and the Hong Kong and Shanghai Bank Building, c. 1930s.

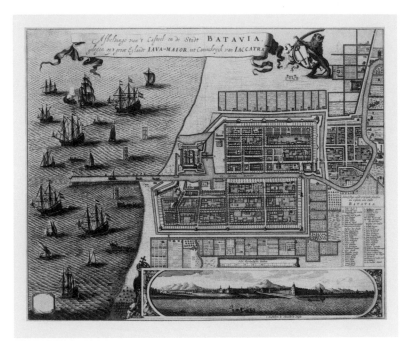

RIGHT: Map of Batavia, 1660s.

— those of Sunda and of Malacca — through which all vessels must pass to reach the city of Canton (today's Guangzhou) and partake of the highly profitable China Trade.

It was precisely to foil the Dutch United East India Company or VOC's (*Vereenigde Oost-Indische Compagnie*) intentions for supremacy over the eastern seas — and therefore their global domination — that the Honourable (English) East India Company pursued a permanent settlement in the Malay Archipelago with much haste and purpose, spurred along by the doughty, persistent and ambitious Sir Stamford Raffles.

On the fateful morning of 29th January 1819, when Raffles finally landed on these shores — purportedly on the very spot at which our visitor is standing taking in the view — he would have been faced with a far more bucolic landscape of huts in the shade of swaying coconut trees. In the near distance, a somewhat larger hut constructed of attap would have stood; this was the Temenggong's residence. From thence would come Major William Farquhar and the Temenggong Abdul Rahman of Johor-Riau, to welcome Raffles ashore and to start the formal proceedings that would settle the question of Singapore.

Farquhar had been dispatched here a few days before Raffles' arrival, to set things in motion. With the Dutch having occupied the port of Rhio, on the island of Bintang in the Riau-Lingga Archipelago (today's Bintan island) — most Singaporeans and visitors don't know that Rhio had been the Honourable Company and Raffles' alternative choice! — Raffles had given instructions that the ancient maritime capital of the Malays, Singapura, be explored.

With an unrivalled harbour and location in the archipelago, and with ancient, mythical credentials to boot, Singapura was the perfect location for a British settlement. An avid scholar of the Malay classics and a romantic at heart, Raffles fancied the Company (and himself) legitimate successors to the empire of Johor-Riau, and saw the Company's occupation of the ruins of ancient Singapura ("the lines of the old city, and its defenses") as a symbol of a New World Order being built on the foundations of the old.

In just eight days after Raffles arrived, the deed was done.

Raffles and the Honourable East India Company signed a Treaty with the newly-anointed Sultan Hussein Shah of Johor-Riau, wherein the latter agreed to cede the settlement of Singapore to the British, in return for his being recognised as the rightful and legitimate heir to the throne of Johor-Riau, and his younger brother, a pretender to the throne. The treaty also called for the sum of 5,000 and 3,000 Spanish dollars per annum to be paid by the Company to Sultan and Temenggung respectively. Most importantly, both parties to the Treaty further agreed not to enter into any other treaty or consent to the settlement of any part of their territory to other European or American powers.

With the treaty signed and sealed, Raffles raised the Union Jack on Singaporean soil, and promptly left the island, leaving Farquhar to administer the new settlement as its First Resident.

A facsimile of the Treaty of Singapore, dated the 6th February 1819, and written in English and Jawi Malay, is displayed in the permanent galleries of today's National Museum of Singapore. Raffles' signature — a hasty scrawl in a not-so-elegant hand — evokes the tense circumstances surrounding the signing of the treaty, in particular, the tactical sleight-of-hand (Sultan Hussein Shah had had to be spirited away secretly from Riau to Singapore to sign the Treaty) involved in securing a British settlement right in the VOC's backyard.

Almost immediately after they gained wind of Raffles' major *coup*, the Dutch clamoured foul play and contended that Raffles had no right to establish settlements in *their* sphere of influence, let alone recognise Sultans. Particularly since they had already identified the younger half-brother to Hussein Shah, the prince Abdul Rahman (to be distinguished from the Temenggong Abdul Rahman) as the legitimate heir to the Johor-Riau throne.

It wasn't until March of 1824 that the Dutch finally, grudgingly, gave up their claim over Singapore. Under the terms of the Anglo-Dutch Treaty signed in London, the Dutch also agreed to relinquish Malacca to the British in exchange for Bencoolen, in Sumatra. The British, in return, promised to respect Dutch supremacy over that part of the Malay Archipelago that would eventually become the Netherlands East Indies and today's Indonesia.

the amount collected from Native
Vessels — The expences of the
Port and the collection of duties
to be defrayed by the British
Government.

درهم حاصل جوكي ايت

Done and concluded at
Singapoora this 6th day
of February in the Year
of Our Lord 1819. answering
to the 11th day of the Month
Rubblelakhir and Year of
the Hejira 1234.

مك درى ايت كبت منوی نك تند
تأثم نسرت جڤ كيت كد واد الم
قوطلس اين
دڤريوان كورت كڤد سبلس هارى
بولن ربيع الاخر تاهن ١٢٣٤
تى سورة دڠكرى كيڤ فى را ات

T.S. Raffles
Agent to the Most
Noble the Gov Genl
with the States of Rhio
Lingen & Johor.

Singapore's fate was secured.

His life's work complete, Raffles lived only two more years. He died of a brain haemorrhage in faraway London in the Summer of 1826, 45 years of age.

Singapore's success lay, in the very beginning, in Raffles' shrewd strategy to declare it a free port.

Up until then, the prevailing approach adopted by the other East India Companies, most notably the Dutch, was monopolistic; in that in Dutch Batavia, only Dutch trading vessels could dock and trade in East Asian goods freely, without any customs or other duties levied. All other vessels were either prohibited from trading, or had heavy customs and other duties slapped on them for the privilege of trade.

Raffles waived customs and other duties for any trading vessel wishing to trade in Singapore. The principle was *freedom to trade*: that any vessel, from anywhere in the world, should have equal opportunity to trade their wares within the limited confines of this particular harbour, as long as there was a market for their goods. This *laissez faire* approach gave Singapore a huge competitive edge almost immediately, as it became the cheapest port to dock at overnight.

Word spread and within three years, Singapore had begun to corner the market, with all manner of trading vessels — European ships, Chinese junks and Malay boats, particularly from Malacca — eager to dock at and trade their wares in its port. Notwithstanding the uncertain circumstances surrounding Singapore — the Anglo-Dutch Treaty would only be signed in 1824 — the Company's investments in the settlement had already begun to bear fruit.

On 12th January 1823, just before he would leave Singapore for the last time in June, Raffles wrote to his cousin, Dr Thomas Raffles (who bore almost the same name), noting that:

> "[t]he progress of my new settlement is in every way most satisfactory, and it would gladden your heart to witness the activity and cheerfulness which prevails throughout. Every day brings us new settlers, and Singapore has already become a great emporium. Houses and warehouses are springing up in every direction, and the inland forests are fast giving way before the industrious cultivator. I am now engaged in marking out the towns and the roads, and in establishing laws and regulations for the protection of person and property. We have no less than nine mercantile houses (European); and there is abundant employment for capital as fast as it accumulates."

OPPOSITE: 1819 Treaty of Singapore between Raffles and the Sultan of Johor.

By the mid-1800s, the free port at Singapore had eclipsed Batavia, and the Dutch themselves had to also declare Batavia a free port, in order for the city to compete. By the turn of the 20th century, Singapore had become the port city *par excellence* in the East Indies, rivalled later by the advent of Hong Kong and Shanghai on the Chinese coast.

Wealth and capital accrued through trade and commerce was invested into building a thoroughly modern city. The earliest parts of the city to be developed were the banks of the Singapore River and the waterfront, which saw houses and warehouses "springing up in every direction". Raffles commissioned a town plan sectioning the city into civic, commercial and ethnic enclaves — an urban configuration that has been preserved in today's Singapore.

Urban planning, engineering and architectural expertise that had gone into building Calcutta as the foremost city of British India was diverted to Singapore, into the construction of a similarly impressive colonial city in Calcutta's image.

On the northern banks of the river sat the government quarter, complete with courthouse and secretariat, and constructed in a Neo-Classical and Palladian style. The entire precinct was christened Empress Place in 1907, in honour of Queen Victoria, Empress of India. Just beside Empress Place, the Esplanade was preserved as a public green flanking the sea, with, on its northern flank, an imposing and impressive row of civic and residential buildings that were successively replaced in later decades with even more monumental buildings, culminating in the Neo-Classical splendour of the Supreme Court and City Hall buildings in the 1920s and '30s.

On the southern bank of the river and along the waterfront, another kind of city emerged. The banks and trading houses — the likes of Jardine, Matheson & Co., Guthrie & Sons, the Hong Kong and Shanghai Bank, and the Chartered Bank of China, India and Australia — erected their mercantile headquarters using the most contemporary technologies and architectural styles of the time. Visitors arriving at Clifford Pier along Collyer Quay in the early 20th century would be awed by the effusive display of architectural styles — not only Neo-Classical but also Renaissance, Moorish and Art Deco — in the Singapore skyline, all of which were eloquent allegories to Trade and Commerce, and spoke of the power and the foresight of the British Empire.

Meanwhile, the city itself expanded landward, with inland jungles cleared for orchards with plantation houses, military cantonments with their "black-and-white" bungalows, and sumptuous villas in sprawling suburban gardens. Networks of roads took modernity deep into the interior, as the population of the island continued to increase exponentially.

Raffles' laws protecting private property and accumulation of wealth drew peoples from all over the globe to the island to seek opportunity; they were not just Britons and other Europeans, but also those of many different races and religions.

In particular, the Chinese came in their thousands from the Eastern coastal ports of the Chinese Mainland. So did the Indians, from the colonial port cities of the British Raj and Ceylon, and the Malays, from all over Nusantara (the Malay Archipelago). In addition, there were Arabs from the arid deserts of the Hadhramaut in Yemen; Jews and Armenians from Baghdad and Isfahan in the Middle East. The result was a cosmopolitan, multi-cultural, polyglot population, one that still describes the population of Singapore today.

Each of these communities left their mark indelibly on the physical urban landscape, in the form of the many different places of worship that they built for spiritual succour — temples, churches, mosques and synagogues; as well as in the form of the unique, vernacular forms of architecture that evolved out of a blending of European and Asian cultures — the ubiquitous Nanyang-style shophouse and the many instances of Eclectic, or hybrid, styles of architecture.

Many of these buildings, along with the communities that continue to live, work and play in them, still stand in contemporary Singapore, and add to the colour and vibrancy of the cityscape.

In 1965, Singapore became an independent Republic after brief stints as a self-governing colony from 1959 to 1963, and as a state of the independent Republic of Malaysia from 1963 to 1965.

In the immediate aftermath of independence, much of the city-state's attention was paid to ensuring that its heritage of trade and commerce, and its position as the foremost trading hub in the region remained unchallenged. Even as ruling authorities decided to retain Raffles — literally, by not pulling down a statue of Raffles that stood at Empress Place — as a symbolic gesture to continuity and to its willingness to do business with the world, large tracts of the city's colonial built heritage were demolished to make way for the creation of yet another incarnation of the thoroughly modern city — the vision of towering glass and steel that our visitor observes across the river from Raffles' landing spot.

It wasn't until the 1980s that, flush with success and affluence, city authorities introduced a programme of built heritage conservation. Since then, there has been a consistent effort to protect historic structures and sites, such that a visitor sightseeing in central Singapore today still finds ample traces of the city's colonial and multi-cultural heritage. In fact, wandering the streets of downtown Singapore, one more often than not stumbles across pockets of architecture frozen in time — areas where a sense of the past still remains strong.

True, much of that which is historic is often juxtaposed against what is startlingly contemporary — one only need recall the warehouses of Boat Quay dwarfed by the towering skyscrapers of Raffles Place. But this seamless marrying of colonial with contemporary is exactly what makes Singapore's cityscape unique. It also renders it very different from other Asian cities.

In recent years, heritage conservation efforts have extended to the realm of intangible heritage, meaning the diversity of cultures, rituals, traditions and forms of arts and leisure of the many ethnic communities in Singapore. Thought is now being placed onto how best to ensure that these more ephemeral traces of the past do not disappear in the pursuit of the contemporary. Certainly, there has been a popular revival of interest in the heritage not just of the largest ethnic communities, the Chinese, Malay and Indian; but also the other smaller, but no less historic, communities.

Natural heritage is also key to discussions of heritage, due in no small part to Singapore's positioning, since the 1980s, as a "Garden City" and more recently, a "City in a Garden". Situated, as it is, on the edge of the equator in the tropical belt, Singapore has one of the largest biodiversities of any city in the world. Raffles and Farquhar acknowledged and were thrilled by this diversity. Much of their time spent in the region was spent doggedly and animatedly collecting natural history specimens and commissioning natural history prints and drawings. Raffles' natural history prints now sit in the vaults of the British Library, while those of Farquhar's are in the collection of the National Museum of Singapore.

This colonial-era interest in flora and fauna perpetuates itself in the city-state and its population's general predilection for parks and greenery. The City's first, and only, UNESCO World Heritage site is a garden — the Singapore Botanic Gardens, established in 1859, but with origins in the Botanical and Experimental Garden Raffles first commissioned on Government Hill (today's Fort Canning) in 1822, and beloved by Singaporeans from all walks of life.

BELOW LEFT: Ship in Tanjong Pagar docks, late 19th century.

BELOW RIGHT: Porcelain shards unearthed from Fort Canning, now on display at the Asian Civilisations Museum.

The colonial being well and properly documented, there has been increasing interest in what came before. Recent archaeological developments have made it possible to piece together a sense of the island's ancient, pre-colonial past — the past that existed before Raffles arrived, and to which he makes reference most evocatively, and on multiple occasions, in his letters.

Writing to the Duchess of Somerset from Penang on 22 February 1819, just after he had concluded the Treaty of Singapore, Raffles notes that:

> *"in [William] Marsden's map of Sumatra you will observe an Island to the north of these straits called Singapura; this is the spot, the site of the ancient maritime capital of the Malays, and within the walls of these fortifications, raised not less than six centuries ago, on which I have planted the British flag, where, I trust, it will long triumphantly wave."*

Since the 1980s, sporadic but sustained archaeological digs on and around Fort Canning and the Singapore River have unearthed a wealth of artefacts dating back to the 14th century. The thousands of shards and fragments of Chinese ceramics dating back to the Yuan Dynasty suggest that there might have already been a trading settlement on the shores of the Singapore River centuries before Europeans arrived.

They corroborate, or at least, appear to corroborate, in a tangible way, Raffles' own knowledge and description of an ancient maritime capital located here. Certainly we know from the *Sejarah Melayu (The Malay Annals)*, the epic history of the Malay peoples that Raffles was also familiar with, that from 1311 to 1411 AD, there was a Kingdom of Singapura that existed right here in the vicinity of the Singapore River and Fort Canning Hill.

We also know that large-scale, trans-oceanic maritime trade already existed in Asia by that time. This is due to the existence of the Belitung Shipwreck, a 9th-century Arab dhow wrecked off the coast of Sumatra which was found carrying Chinese ceramics and other luxury items from Tang China. Its precious cargo is today displayed in the permanent galleries of the Asian Civilisations Museum, located just beside the white statue of Raffles where our visitor continues to stand, gazing across the water to Boat Quay.

If indeed China was trading by sea with the rest of Asia by the time of the first Malay Kings, one of the most logical and efficient trading routes would have been round the tip of the Malay peninsula and north up the Straits of Malacca to the Indian Ocean. Along the way, it is entirely conceivable that some of these vessels would have stopped off at the Kingdom of Singapura to unload some of their precious cargo.

In all likelihood, therefore, Singapore's history as some kind of port city and entrepôt possibly predates its establishment by Raffles by about four if not six centuries (as Raffles posited).

BELOW: Map of the Straits Settlements, late 19th century.

This suggestion of ancient-ness adds a heady dash of epic romance to Singapore's already rich, colourful and multi-layered history and heritage.

Welcome to Singapore, and this book about its history and heritage.

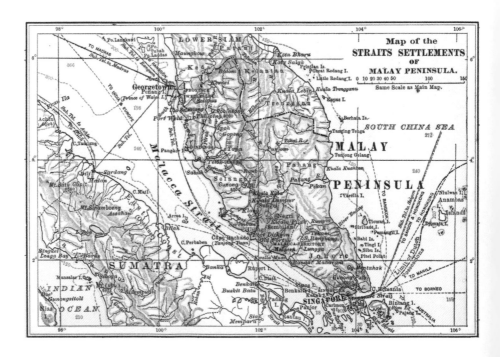

Singapore River and Government Hill.
Lithograph, by Edwin Augustus Porcher,
Vincent Brooks (engraver). 1850s.

CHAPTER ONE

PEOPLE & PLACES

FORBIDDEN HILL

"After a long time, when his earthly period was completed, Sri Tri-buana departed his life, and was buried on the hill of Singhapura…"

— *The Malay Annals* (1400s),
translated by John Leyden (1821)

One of the oldest and most historic places in Singapore is a gentle knoll that sits at the edge of the harbour and, for centuries, has been a defining landmark of the island's skyline. Today, it is known as Fort Canning Hill, after Viscount Charles John Canning (1812–1862), who was the Governor-General and subsequently the first Viceroy of British India from 1856 to 1862. But, for centuries, it was known by the native Malays as *Bukit Larangan* or 'Forbidden Hill' and it was a place steeped in myth and mysticism.

The hill was forbidden to the everyman for two reasons. Firstly, it was regarded as a royal precinct. The Malays believed that the hill had been the seat of local royalty, and indeed, *The Malay Annals* or *Sejarah Melayu*, a 14th-century epic history of the Malay Kings, tell of a palace that used to stand on the hill, and had stood there for some two centuries until the Portuguese came in the 1500s and demolished it. Secondly, the hill was a sacred precinct: it was believed that this was the final resting place of Sang Nila Utama, the first Raja and founder of Singapura (the Malay name for Singapore). Even today, a mysterious *keramat* or shrine sits along the foot-hills of the precinct. It is ostensibly dedicated to Iskander Shah, the last king of Singapura and Sang Nila Utama's descendant, who, in 1411, fled to Malacca to establish the mighty Malacca Sultanate.

Scholars have suggested that the shrine could not possibly hold Iskander Shah's remains, since historical accounts have him passing away in the great city of Malacca, in the empire that he created. Some believe the *keramat* could possibly hold the remains of Sang Nila Utama himself.

Whatever the case, the *keramat* holds a very deep and profound place in local Malay belief, and it continues to be closely watched and guarded by a self-appointed member of the local community.

OPPOSITE: Sir Thomas Stamford Bingley Raffles by George Francis Joseph. Oil on Canvas. 1817.

When the British arrived in 1819, they established a residence atop the hill, no doubt recognising the significance of the place to the local Malays and understanding also that to establish legitimacy as the new rulers of Singapore, they had to occupy this important landmark.

Bukit Larangan became Government Hill, and the first Briton to take up residence atop that hill was none other than Sir Thomas Stamford Raffles himself. In a letter to William Marsden in 1823, Raffles acknowledged the sacredness and the rarefied environs of the hill, and in an offhand manner, described his own position with regards to the Malay Kings:

"We have lately built a small bungalow on Singapore Hill where, though the height is inconsiderable, we find a great difference in climate. Nothing can be more interesting and beautiful than the view from this spot. The tombs of the Malay Kings are close at hand, and I have settled that if it is my fate to die here I shall take my place amongst them...".

Here on the hill, Raffles also established the city's first botanical gardens in 1822. And, in keeping with the sacredness and sanctity of the hill, a Christian cemetery for the early British settlers in Singapore was created on its slopes in 1846.

By 1859, faced with the increasing threat of a maritime attack, the British Colonial Government decided to build a military fortress and garrison on Government Hill. The governors' residence was demolished, the Botanical Gardens relocated, and in their place were established the barracks and other associated structures that continue to be landmarks today.

Fort Canning Hill served as the headquarters of the British Army up until 1963, save during the intervening years of the Japanese Occupation (1942–1945) during which time the Japanese also used the Fort as their military quarters. It remained a military precinct until the late 1970s, when it was finally decommissioned and turned into a public park.

But its history does not end there.

In the mid-1980s, archaeological excavations, commissioned by the National Museum of Singapore with the intent of establishing tangible proof to the legend of the Malay Kings, uncovered an astonishing trove of porcelain shards, glass beads and other paraphernalia dating from the 14th century. Earlier in 1926, the British, in the course of building a reservoir atop Fort Canning Hill, had uncovered a small trove of Majapahit-era (14th-century) gold.

These findings afforded some weight to the long-standing myth of Bukit Larangan or Forbidden Hill.

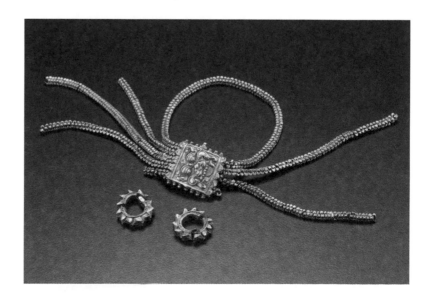

OPPOSITE: *View of Singapore from Government Hill* by John Turnbull Thomson. Lithograph. 1846.

RIGHT: Gold armlet and earrings — the so-called "Majapahit Gold", 14th century.

"Then Sang Nila Utama reached a stone of great height and size, in which he mounted and viewed the opposite shore, with its sands white as cotton; and enquiring what sands were these which he saw, Indra B'hupala informed him they were the sands of the extensive country of Tamasak. The prince immediately proposed to visit them, and the minister agreeing, they went immediately on shipboard."

—The Malay Annals (1400s),
translated by John Leyden (1821)

To better understand the mysticism surrounding Bukit Larangan, some back story is in order.

An ancient and very popular legend in Singapore has the island founded in 1299 by Sang Nila Utama, a Hindu Prince of the Srivijayan Empire. Leaving his home city of Palembang in what is today's Sumatra, the prince arrives in the many islands of the Riau Archipelago. Intrigued by one particular island at the tip of the Malayan Peninsula, he enquires as to its name, and is told that it is the island of "Temasek" meaning a little "sea town".

En route to the island, a storm breaks and the seas become tumultuous. The ship that carries Sang Nila Utama threatens to sink. The men on board

RIGHT: Map of the island of Sumatra and the Malayan Peninsula. The approximate area of the Malacca Sultanate encompassed Malaya and the north-eastern shore of Sumatra closest to Malaya. Sebastian Münster. Woodblock print. Mid-1500s.

RIGHT: Headless horseman from Empress Place Archaeological site, c. 14th century.

throw all heavy objects overboard but to no avail. It is only when the prince throws aboard his golden crown — and, some say, also a human sacrifice — that the waters subside and the storm dies down.

Landing on the island, Sang Nila Utama disembarks and heads into the forest to hunt. He chances upon a strange and beautiful creature — its body of a red colour, its head black and its breast white — that he is told is a lion. Determining that the presence of the lion is a good omen, he renames the island "Singapura" or "Lion City", and decides to establish a new kingdom at the mouth of the Singapore River.

Sang Nila Utama would rule the Kingdom of Singapura for half a century (1299–1347). And when he passed, he was buried, so *The Malay Annals* recount, in the foothills of Bukit Larangan.

In *The Malay Annals*, Sang Nila Utama is referred to by his official Javanese honorific — *Sri Maharaja Sang Utama Parameswara Batara Sri Tri Buana* or *Sri Tri Buana* for short, meaning the "Lord King of the three worlds of Palembang, Bintan and Singapura". He was succeeded by four other Rajas: Sri Wikrama Wira (1347–1362), Sri Rana Wikrama (1362–1375), Sri Maharajah (1375–1389), and finally, Parameswara (1389–1398). All were purportedly buried in the sacred precinct of Bukit Larangan.

The last King of Singapura flees his kingdom in the wake of an attack by the Majapahit Empire, which had supplanted the Srivijayan Empire in Sumatra. He founds a new city-state in Malacca, and purportedly converts to Islam, changing his name to Iskander Shah ("Iskander" is the Persian variant of "Alexander" and is also a reference to Alexander the Great). Meanwhile, the Kingdom of Singapura fades into obscurity, 100 years after it was founded.

THE SINGAPORE STONE

"On the stony point which forms the western side of the entrance of the salt creek, on which the modern town of Singapore is building, there was discovered, two years ago, a tolerably hard block of sand-stone, with an inscription upon it. [...] It is upon the inner surface of the stone that the inscription is engraved. The workmanship is far ruder than anything of the kind that I have seen in Java or India; and the writing, perhaps from time, in some degree, but more from the natural decomposition of the rock, so much obliterated as to be quite illegible as a composition. Here and there, however, a few letters seem distinct enough."

— John Crawfurd, *Journal of an Embassy from the Governor-General of India to the Courts of Siam and Cochin China*, 1828.

One of the most mysterious objects from Singapore's past, reverently displayed in the permanent galleries of the National Museum of Singapore, is a hunk of sandstone known as the Singapore Stone. It dates from antiquity, bearing on it a strange script, still undeciphered, but probably related to Old Javanese.

Legend goes that during the reign of Sri Rana Wikrama (1362–1375), a young man by the name of Badang arrived in the Kingdom of Singapura and, in the royal courts, gave a demonstration of his super-human strength. In those days, a large rock stood before the Royal Palace; and as a means of entertaining the King, warriors from across Singapura were challenged to lift the rock above their heads. Badang succeeded where others before him had failed, lifting the rock high above his head and tossing it into the sea near the mouth of the Singapura River.

RIGHT: Singapore Stone, 10th–14th century.

The rock would stand on a tiny promontory jutting out into the Singapore Straits, and forming a narrow passageway for vessels wishing to enter the Singapore River. The British called this promontory (and the rock) Rocky Point and its location was approximately where the Fullerton Building stands today.

Unfortunately, in order to widen the approach to the harbour, the British blew up the Rock in 1843. Thereafter, the best remaining pieces of the Rock with the most intelligible tracts of writing were sent to the Indian Museum in Calcutta. But one fragment returned to Singapore and was later taken into the Raffles Library and Museum, where it remains today.

THE LEGEND OF RADEN MAS

Old Singapore wasn't just the preserve of men. Besides tales of mythical kings and warriors, there was also one of a beautiful princess.

Legend goes that in a Kingdom in Java there was once a handsome and much loved Prince, the brother of a Sultan of that Kingdom at the time. Against his brother, the Sultan's, wishes, the Prince took a commoner as his wife — a beautiful palace dancer he had met and fallen in love with during a celebration at the court.

Together, they had a daughter so lovely that they named her Raden Mas Ayu or "Princess Gold" (*Raden Ayu* is a Javanese honorific used by female nobility). But their happiness was short-lived as the Sultan, incensed at his brother's disobedience, had his brother's wife, the beautiful dancer, killed.

With the help of a loyal servant, the Prince fled to Singapura with his young daughter, the Princess Mas. There, they were welcomed heartily by the Sultan of Singapura and they settled down in the Telok Blangah area, at the foot of what is today Mount Faber.

BELOW: Keramat Puteri Radin Mas Ayu.

The Prince eventually remarried, this time to a princess of the house of Singapura. Jealous of her husband's love for his daughter, she schemed to have Raden Mas Ayu married off to her evil nephew. The plot was foiled in a dramatic fashion. As the evil nephew attempted to stab the old Prince with his *keris*, Raden Mas Ayu stepped in to defend her father, receiving the fatal blow and dying in her father's arms.

Raden Mas Ayu was buried near her home in Telok Blangah, at the foot of Telok Blangah Hill (renamed Mount Faber later on). Today, a shrine or *keramat* still stands at the spot where she is supposedly buried. It is painted yellow and green, to symbolise royalty in the Malay tradition and holiness in Islamic tradition, and it is visited by a small number of devotees of all races wishing to pay their respects. The larger precinct in which her shrine sits, and in which she had lived with her father is also named Radin Mas ("Golden Princess"), in her honour.

RIGHT: Thomas Stamford Raffles. Engraving. 1824.

SIR THOMAS STAMFORD RAFFLES: THE MAN AND HIS LEGACY

"Let the commercial interests for the present drop every idea of a direct trade to China, and let them concentrate their influence in supporting Singapore, and they will do ten times better. As a free port, it is as much to them as the possession of Macao; and it is here their voyages should finish. [...] Singapore may, as a free port, thus become the connecting link and grand entrepot between Europe, Asia and China; it is, in fact, fast becoming so."

— Letter from Raffles to the Reverend
Dr Raffles, Bencoolen, 17th July 1820.

There is no single personage more associated with Singapore than Raffles, or to be specific, Sir Thomas Stamford Bingley Raffles (1781–1826). Born on a ship off the coast of Jamaica, he gained employment with the British East India Company at the ripe young age of 14, and for the next 30 years, sought to distinguish himself in the port cities of colonial Southeast Asia.

While the founding of modern Singapore is his main claim to fame, his contributions elsewhere in Southeast Asia are no less significant.

He began his career in the colonial service as Assistant Secretary to the Governor of Penang in 1805. Two years later, sailing into the nearby colony of Malacca, which had briefly shifted from Dutch to British hands in the wake of the Napoleonic Wars, he put a stop to the British army's wanton destruction of the city's 16th-century Portuguese walls. The sole remaining section of the wall — known as *La Porta de Santiago* or *A Famosa* — still stands today in Malacca, and is a testament to his ambition and desire to leave a legacy.

A strong command of the Malay language and a willingness to research local customs put Raffles in good stead with the Governor-General of British India at the time, the Lord Minto (1751–1814; governorship 1807–1813). Demonstrating his mastery of strategy, Raffles suggested that Lord Minto use the Napoleonic Wars as an excuse to seize territory in the Netherlands East Indies, most notably the island of Java. The invasion was carried through and Britain successfully wrested Java from the Dutch after a mere 45-day siege.

Raffles was made Lieutenant-Governor of the island, and moved to its capital Batavia (today's Jakarta). He was there only until 1815, when Java reverted to the Dutch.

Raffles wasted no time in these critical four years. Amongst his achievements were the comprehensive research and documentation of Java's ancient monuments, including the Hindu temple of Prambanan and the Buddhist temple-mountain of Borobudur. He also wrote and oversaw the publication of a monumental work of scholarship, *The History of Java*. The brief British period he presided over saw further tremendous shifts in fashion, styles of interior decor and social behaviour. For example, where the Dutch had preferred entertaining themselves and their friends in the privacy of their own homes, Raffles introduced that quintessential British institution — the ball — and encouraged public cultural pursuits such as museum- and theatre-going.

For his achievements in Java, Raffles was accorded a knighthood in 1817 by none other than the Prince Regent (the future George IV). And in true Regency-era fashion, he had a portrait of himself commissioned by a rather fashionable portrait painter at the time, George Francis Joseph (1764–1846).

The Portrait of Sir Thomas Stamford Bingley Raffles is the most iconic portrait of him in oil on canvas. It hangs today in the National Portrait Gallery in London, though a copy of the portrait, commissioned in 1912 by the local Colonial Government, hangs today in the National Museum of Singapore. In the rather stirring and life-like portrait, Raffles is set against a backdrop of tropical Javanese jungle, surrounded by objects and papers that allude to his achievements in Java. He sits calmly and with a self-consciously regal air, as if to say: "I have arrived". Although, as history would have it, his greatest achievement had yet to come at the time.

After Java, Raffles was appointed to the far less prestigious position of Governor-General of Bencoolen. Bencoolen, or Bengkulu, was a small trading city situated on the southern coast of the island of Sumatra. It was a backwater in the East Indies, ill-fitted to Raffles' grand ambitions. As Raffles set about diligently organising and administrating the colony in accordance with his duties, he continued to explore the region, his heart set on a bigger prize.

In 1819, after surveying the islands around the Riau Archipelago, he settled on a small island at the tip of the Malay Peninsula, which was known as Singapura or "Lion City". A shrewd tactician and negotiator, Raffles took advantage of a crisis of succession in the ruling Johor-Riau Sultanate to persuade the rightful Crown Prince, Hussein Shah, to cede the island of Singapore to the East India Company in return for the Company recognising him as legitimate heir to the throne.

The strategy worked. On 6 February 1819, Singapore became British, and, having achieved his goal, Raffles left the very next day, leaving the administration of the island to its appointed First Resident, Major William Farquhar.

Over the course of the next three years, Raffles continued to spend his time in Bencoolen, returning only sporadically to Singapore to see how the fledgling colony was getting on. All in all, he probably spent no more than ten months in the colony in total; but in typical prolific fashion, he managed to commission the colony's first town plan, write the colony's first constitution, found the colony's first European-style school (the Raffles Institution) and establish a Botanical and Experimental Garden at the foot of Government Hill.

In February 1824, he boarded a ship in Bencoolen bound ultimately for England. The vessel, called the *Fame*, would ironically become infamous for having caught fire and sunk, taking with it all of Raffles' personal effects, a lifetime of research and his extensive collection of natural history specimens. He attempted to replace part of this research in the course of the next two years, but sadly died in London of a brain haemorrhage on 5th July 1826, a mere 45 years of age.

Despite Raffles barely being in Singapore during his lifetime, he became immortalised as the city's founder. Much of his initial fame was attributed

to the memoir his widow, Sophia Hull-Raffles, wrote in the years following his death. Entitled *Memoir of the Life and Public Services of Sir Stamford Raffles F. R. S. Etc, Particularly in the Government of Java, 1811–1816, and of Bencoolen and its Dependencies, 1817–1824; with Details of the Commerce and Resources of the Eastern Archipelago, and Selections from his Correspondence*, it contained many of Raffles' letters and reports, speeches and memos and continues to be one of the most comprehensive first-hand biographies of the man. In particular, the memoir attributes the founding of Singapore to Raffles and Raffles alone, ignoring the significant part others, such as William Farquhar, had played.

In Singapore, Raffles would be remembered and celebrated by colonial authorities and business people alike. In 1858, Commercial Square, the colony's banking and trading quarter, was renamed Raffles Place in his honour; a name the square still bears today. In 1887, the Raffles Library and Museum and the Raffles Hotel were also established, in memory of his name. In 1887, to commemorate Queen Victoria's Golden Jubilee, a statue of Raffles was commissioned and placed first at the Esplanade, and then moved, in 1919, to the forecourt of the Victoria Memorial Hall to commemorate the centenary of Singapore's founding.

Contemporary Singapore continues to honour and commemorate its founding father, affording him an almost reverential place in its national consciousness. Raffles' name is so inextricably linked to Singapore as to adorn many of its streets, squares, skyscrapers, schools, hotels, hospitals and even companies. In fact, through a shrewd strategy of tourism and nation-branding, the name "Raffles" itself has become almost synonymous with Singapore world-wide — a global and highly recognisable brand worthy of the great commercial emporium Singapore became and continues to be today.

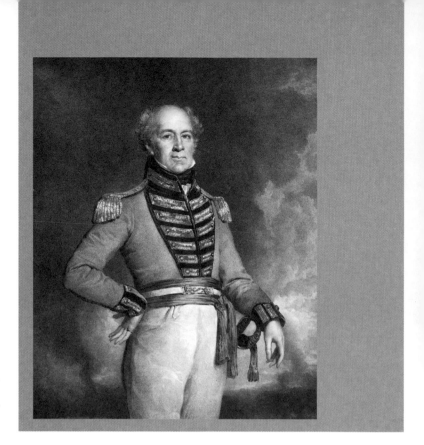

RIGHT: Portrait of William
Farquhar by M. Gauci,
after John Graham-Gilbert.
Lithograph. 1830.

WILLIAM FARQUHAR, FIRST RESIDENT OF SINGAPORE

*"I will now return to the story of how Col. Farquhar sailed away in a ship. He
ordered the ship to steer towards the Straits of Singapore; and the reason why
he went there was that for a long time he had been friendly with Tengku Long,
the son of Sultan Mahmud, at the time when he was at Malacca; and I heard
it said that Tengku Long had received some money from Col. Farquhar. At
that very time he had promised to give the island of Singapore to the English.
Moreover, Mr. Farquhar had been to Riau to meet with him, in order to enter
into such an agreement with him, and when the agreement had been made, he
then returned to hand the town over to the Dutch as I have described."*

— *The Autobiography of Munshi Abdullah* (1849),
translated by Reverend W G Shellabear (1918)

Unlike Stamford Raffles, who secured a permanent place in Singapore's
popular consciousness, William Farquhar, who was arguably as important
to the founding of Singapore as Raffles, is strangely absent from Singapore's
efforts to commemorate its colonial past.

Major William Farquhar (1774–1839, pronounced "FAR-Ker"), First British Resident of Singapore, was a Scotsman, born in the Highlands of Aberdeenshire. Like Raffles, he started his career with the East India Company at a very young age and rose through the ranks through stints in British India.

Farquhar's big break came in 1795, when he took part in the successful military campaign to wrest the city of Malacca from the Dutch (while the Napoleonic Wars were sweeping over Europe). Farquhar was promoted to a full Major in 1811, and made Resident and Commandant of Malacca, a post he would hold until the city was returned to the Dutch in 1818.

With his extensive knowledge of Malaya, he was fortunate to have made the acquaintance of Raffles, by whom he was asked to search for a possible new British settlement in the Malay Archipelago. Raffles had strategically assessed, in the wake of Malacca's reversion to the Dutch, that a stronger British presence in the East Indies would be critical to ensuring a balance of power in the East and to preventing the Dutch from exerting a monopoly and stranglehold on trade to and from China.

As Raffles' emissary, Farquhar assisted in negotiations with the Temenggong (a sort of local Chief of Defence) of Singapura, drafting up the Treaty of Friendship and Alliance that would eventually be signed by Raffles, the Temenggong, and Tengku Long (later to be Sultan Hussein Shah of Johor) — the very treaty which ceded Singapore to the East India Company on 6th February 1819.

With Singapore secured, Raffles appointed Farquhar First British Resident and Commandant of the colony, with responsibility to organise, develop and administer the settlement in accordance with plans that Raffles had scrupulously drawn up. Somewhat less of a stickler for orderliness than Raffles (who was admittedly rather puritanical in outlook), Farquhar decided instead to largely ignore the plan, and allow the colony to develop in a more organic fashion.

The initial years saw Singapore grow and thrive, with traders, merchants and other less salubrious types bringing their business and vice to these shores. Farquhar cleared the banks of the Singapore River to enable the establishment of commercial and residential quarters. And when he ran out of money in the Treasury, he allowed for the establishment of gambling dens and auctioned off monopoly rights to sell opium and alcohol.

Naturally, when Raffles returned to Singapore in 1822 after an absence of more than two years, he was appalled by the messiness of the colony, and livid that his well-intentioned plans had not been implemented. Raffles and Farquhar had a falling out, with the former having the latter summarily dismissed from his position in mid 1823. By the end of that same year, Farquhar left Singapore for good, much to the chagrin of the local European, Malay and Chinese communities who had been very fond of him during his tenure. He died back in Scotland in 1839, at the age of 66.

Farquhar's legacy in Singapore remains tenuous, since the Town Plan that Raffles subsequently commissioned and implemented superseded much of what he might have achieved by way of urban planning. He is remembered today primarily through a series of 477 paintings of the flora and fauna of Malacca and Singapore, which Farquhar commissioned during his time as First Resident of Singapore, and which resides today in the halls of the National Museum of Singapore.

THE JACKSON PLAN

The Jackson Plan, also known as the Plan of the Town of Singapore, was the colony's first town plan and is the earliest known map of modern Singapore. Commissioned by Stamford Raffles in 1822, it was a response to the rather more laissez-faire manner in which William Farquhar had allowed Singapore to develop in its initial years.

Raffles preferred things to be orderly, and the plan reflects this penchant for putting things in their right place. The settlement that Raffles envisioned was organised by land-use, with civic, military, commercial and residential quarters each having their proper place in the settlement. The map also called for segregation of the races, with the Europeans, Malay-Muslims, Chinese and Indian (known then as Klings or Chuliahs, depending on whether they were Hindu or Muslim) each having their respective "campongs" or ethnic quarters.

The plan is known as the Jackson Plan, after Lieutenant Philip Jackson (1802–1879), who was the colony's earliest engineer and land surveyor. In drawing up the plan, Jackson (and Raffles) had had a long tradition of urban planning to take reference from, in particular the specific tradition of segregated urban planning in the major cities of British India — Madras (Chennai), Bombay (Mumbai) and Calcutta (Kolkata), the latter being the capital of British India from 1772 to 1911.

In Calcutta, the Europeans were settled in the so-called "White Town", occupying higher ground, and land that was more favourable. The local Bengali population was settled somewhat further out from the city centre, in their own "Black Town", which was self-contained and had its own commercial and religious quarters. In between "white" and "black" towns grew a kind of grey area or "grey town", so to speak, where the city's other immigrant races settled. These included the Chinese, especially, but also Muslim-Arab communities, the Parsis, the Jews, the Armenians and the Anglo-Indians (Eurasians).

This clear segregation — drawn from the heritage of British India — is reflected in the Jackson Plan. "White Town" occupies the north bank of the Singapore River, including a civic district centred on the "Open Square" as well as a residential district to the north. The equivalent of "Black Town" is

OPPOSITE: The Jackson Plan, oriented with north to the top of the page, 1828.

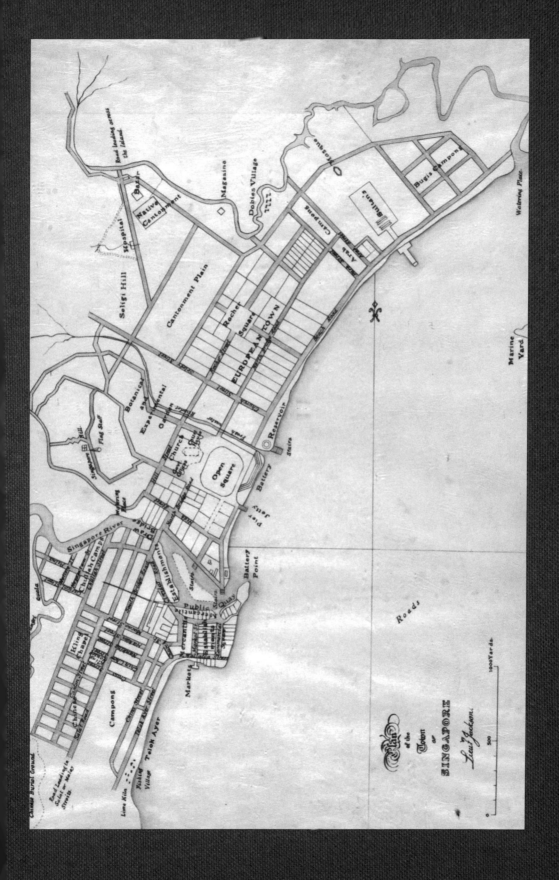

situated in and around the royal precinct centred on the Sultan of Johor's Palace and Mosque. It incorporates specific "campongs" for Arab Muslims and the seafaring Bugis.

"Grey town" was relegated to the area of Telok Ayer, south of the Singapore River, and marked "Chinese campong" and "Kling campong" on the map. Later on, however, a sort of grey area would also emerge in between European Town and the royal precinct, with Chinese and Indian communities living and worshipping side by side.

The wonderful thing about the Jackson Plan is that two centuries on, its basic planning parameters are still more or less apparent in the urban plan of downtown Singapore. European town is today's Civic District and Bras Basah precincts, with their concentration of some of the oldest and most majestic colonial-era civic, cultural and religious institutions in Singapore. At the eastern edges of the Bras Basah precinct where it abuts the Malay quarter, a sort of grey area with Chinese and Hindu temples, a Jewish synagogue and Armenian Church still exists, with thriving communities of worshippers.

The Royal precinct, or Malay Quarter is today's Kampong Gelam. It continues to be a centre of Malay-Muslim culture, cuisine and business; at its heart is the former Sultan's Palace (transformed into a museum of Malay Heritage) and the Sultan Mosque.

Meanwhile, the Telok Ayer area is regarded as Singapore's Chinatown and still maintains a strong presence of traditional Chinese businesses. While the Indian community has largely decamped to their own Little India quarter in Serangoon, the presence of two major places of worship — the Sri Mariamman Temple and the Masjid Jamae (Chulia) — hint at the former "Kling campong", and in any case still cater to the religious needs of Hindus and Indian Muslims alike.

All in all, Raffles would be pleased at how orderly his city centre has been and how his legacy lives on today.

THE SINGAPORE RIVER AND ITS ENVIRONS

"On the side towards the river there were four or five little huts, and there were six or seven cocoanut trees which had been planted there; and there was one house a little larger, but also built of atap, which was where the Temenggong lived. Mr Farquhar walked all round the Esplanade, and the sea gypsies (Orang Laut) came and looked at him, and then ran and told the Temenggong."

— *The Autobiography of Munshi Abdullah* (1849),
translated by Reverend W G Shellabear (1918)

The Singapore River, or the Sungei Singapura, doesn't have quite the same pedigree as the other great rivers of the world — the Ganges, the Nile, the Thames and the Seine — with their thousands of years of bankside civilisation. Nor is it quite as voluminous a water body as these other giants, being of a rather more modest scale — a creek, really, coursing its bucolic way from the gentle knolls of central Singapore out into the Singapore Straits.

It is, however, a rather important river, insofar as it has witnessed the development of a great global emporium-city along its shores, and continues to be the entry point to a deeper understanding of the history and heritage of this emporium-city.

The earliest mention of the Sungei Singapura probably dates from the 13th century. The *Sejarah Melayu* observes the existence of a fishing settlement, Temasek, at the mouth of the River. Thereafter, it notes that the name of the settlement was changed to Singapura ("Lion City"), and that royal compounds and a royal dynasty were established at the foot of the hill, to the north of the river.

The most likely inhabitants of the city at the time were the Orang Laut, the "Sea Gypsies" of the Malay world, who, for centuries, have plied the

RIGHT: Boat Quay, early 20th century.

RIGHT: Singapore River with native craft, early 20th century.

waters all across the Malay Archipelago, living their entire lives on the water, in houseboats and houses on stilts. Certainly, when Stamford Raffles came to Singapura with his entourage, the largest residential community in the island would have been the Orang Laut, and they existed in Singapore up until the 1970s, when they were resettled onto dry land.

From 1819, the humble mouth of the Singapore River served as a free port, welcoming ships and sailing vessels from all over world. As Singapore developed into a thriving, cosmopolitan capital of trade and commerce in the course of the 1800s, so did the nature of ships docking at the mouth of the river become more fabulous. There were junks from the many glittering coastal ports of China and Indochina; *pnisis* and *perahus* from Java, Bugis and Sumatra; and steamships from India, the Middle East and Great Britain. As they docked by the slender jetties along the river mouth, they disgorged onto the shore thousands of peoples from all around Asia and the world — coolies, merchant traders, civil servants, and more. Their descendents make up Singapore's multicultural population today.

On both banks of the river — north and south — were built row upon row of low-rise warehouses or godowns (a word of South Indian origin), that served to store the large quantities and huge variety of goods brought from all over the world to Singapore's shores. Many of the goods were only stored temporarily, and were swiftly re-exported. From early on in its history, the colonial authorities had adopted a shrewd strategy of positioning Singapore as an entrepôt or a centre where goods were imported only to be swiftly exported again. Entrepôt trade and free port status, with all ships and sailing vessels docking in Singapore exempt from taxes and duties, combined to make Singapore one of the most bustling and commercially successful ports in the region.

In the 1860s, as shipping technologies advanced and as the ships themselves became bigger and more frequent, it became apparent that the Singapore River was inadequate and a new, larger port needed to be built to accommodate ships of a larger tonnage. Much of the shipping was diverted to the New Harbour, renamed Keppel Harbour in 1900. But the Singapore River continued to receive trading vessels of a smaller variety up until the mid 1900s.

For much of Singapore's history, the most iconic views of Singapore have been those taken of the river and its environs. In the early 1900s, in particular, photographs and postcards depicted alternating views of imposing edifices in Neo-Classical and Palladian styles on the north bank of the river; and views of the rows of godowns on the south bank, fronted by hundreds of houseboats floating on the water, home to the Chinese and Malay boat-people.

All trading activity of a maritime nature was finally excised from the Singapore River in the late 1970s by the Singaporean Government. A massive exercise to clean up the pollution in the river ensued in the 1980s. This was followed by a major effort to conserve, restore and re-purpose the buildings along the riverbanks. The various quays — Boat, Clarke and Robertson Quays — were transformed into lifestyle and residential precincts, while a brand new, towering Financial District sprung up at the mouth of the river itself.

Today's Singapore River is again home to a bustling and cosmopolitan commercial and residential centre, though in place of the many merchants and the trading houses of yore, we have the Asian headquarters of some of the world's biggest banks and financial institutions; and in place of the houseboats, godowns and coolies, we have a glittering array of restaurants, pubs and shopping establishments catering to a new breed of international migrants — young, upwardly mobile professionals working in the towering skyscrapers of the global financial industry.

Historic Bridges across the Singapore River

More than ten individual bridges span the Singapore River. Of these, seven were built in the colonial period, and each of them was named after a significant personage in colonial history. All but one of these "personality bridges" still exists in its original form and they are listed below in the order they were built.

The oldest of the "personality bridges", and ironically also the youngest, is Coleman Bridge. First built as a brick bridge in 1840 (and the second bridge to be built across the river), it was designed by George Drumgold Coleman, the most important architect in the initial decades of Singapore's founding. This bridge was later replaced with a timber one in 1865 and subsequently a metal one in 1886. Unfortunately, it was demolished in 1986, in order to cope with increasing traffic, and replaced with the present concrete bridge in 1990.

The oldest bridge *still existing in its original form* is Cavenagh Bridge, constructed in 1869 and named after Major William Orfeur Cavenagh (1821–1891), Governor of the Straits Settlements from 1859 to 1867, and the final one to be appointed by the East India Company. The only suspension bridge over the river, its component parts had been constructed in Glasgow, Scotland and shipped over to Singapore to be assembled here by Indian convicts.

Ord Bridge, completed in 1886, is the next oldest extant bridge. It is a steel truss bridge, named after Colonel Sir Harry St George Ord (1819–1885) who followed Cavenagh as Governor of the Straits Settlements from 1867 to 1873 and was the first Governor to be appointed after the Settlements had become a Crown Colony. The bridge is also known as Ordnance Bridge or Toddy Bridge due to neighbouring ordnance stores and shops in the old days selling "toddy" or illegal, homemade spirits. These are, naturally, all gone today.

Read Bridge was completed in 1889. It was named after Scotsman, William Henry Macleod Read (1819–1909), a very prominent citizen in the colony and the first non-government Member of Parliament to make notable contributions to public service.

It was followed by Anderson Bridge in 1910, named after Sir John Anderson (1858–1918), Governor of the Straits Settlements and High Commissioner for the Federated Malay States from 1904 to 1911. The bridge was built to take the traffic load off Cavenagh Bridge and it is still heavily plied by vehicular traffic.

Clemenceau Bridge, completed in 1920, was named after former French Prime Minister Georges Clemenceau (1841–1929), who had been in town to attend the groundbreaking ceremony of the Cenotaph. The latter had been erected in the memory of British troops who had lost their lives in World War I.

Finally, there is Elgin Bridge, built in 1929. It was named after Lord Elgin (1811–1863), Governor-General of British India from 1862 to 1863. He had been infamous for having ordered the sack of the Summer Palace in Beijing and, on a related note, was also the son of the earlier, equally infamous Lord Elgin who had commandeered the Elgin Marbles. Elgin Bridge replaced earlier versions of the same dating back to 1863; as well as an even earlier Presentiment Bridge, the very first bridge to be built across the Singapore River.

BELOW LEFT: Cavenagh Bridge, early 20th century.

BELOW RIGHT: Elgin Bridge, early 20th century.

The Esplanade

At the heart of Raffles' town plan for Singapore was a large public space and green area that flanked the sea. Noted simply as the "Open Square" on the town plan, this large public space became known later on as the Esplanade.

For the English, an "esplanade" referred to a long, flat and open area next to a water body, whether it be the sea or a river. It was a man-made public space built to allow pedestrians to promenade without getting their feet dirty in sand or gravel, and to be a recreation ground for sporting and leisure activities. The American equivalent of "esplanade" is a "boardwalk", while the French called their esplanades "corniches".

Esplanades became very popular in the Victorian era, particularly in seaside resorts such as Blackpool, Brighton and Hastings, where visitors would stroll in their fashionable best to see and be seen. The British (and other colonial powers) exported the form of the esplanade to the various capital cities of their colonies abroad. Some of the most famous esplanades in the world include Marine Drive in Bombay, the Corniche in Beirut and Roxas Boulevard along Manila Bay.

In form, the Esplanade in Singapore most resembles the esplanades in British India, which were also known by another name — Maidans. A maidan, Hindi for "open field" (though the word "maidan" has Persian ori-

BELOW: *The Esplanade from Scandal Point*, by John Turnbull Thomson. Oil on canvas. 1851.

gins), wasn't only a waterfront promenade but was also a cricket green, a space for social gatherings on special occasions, and a venue for military parades. On one flank of the maidan would be the most opulent and imposing civic monuments in the city, while on the other flank would be the sea (or the river).

This is certainly the basic form of two of the most famous Maidans in the world — the Oval Maidan in Bombay and the Maidan at Chowringhee, Calcutta — at least until land reclamation extended the shoreline further out into the sea and the Maidans no longer clung to the waterfront. Another iconic maidan (and esplanade), the Galle Face Green in Colombo, continues to sit just off the waterfront, allowing for a leisurely promenade affording stunning views of the Indian Ocean.

As in British India, Singapore's Maidan was the centre of public life in the fledgling colony. In Malay, it was known as the *Padang Besar* or "large open field". Today, it is known formally as the Padang, though throughout its lifetime, the field has been variously called the Esplanade, the Plain, Raffles' Plain, Cantonment Plain and so on.

In its early colonial-era heyday, the Esplanade is best captured in a painting by John Turnbull Thomson (1821–1884) called *The Esplanade from Scandal Point* (see opposite). Painted in 1851, it hangs in the National Museum of Singapore today. The painting is composed from the point of view of one standing on the waterfront looking inland. It depicts a cross-section of colonial society in the 1850s, from the sea gypsies or Orang Laut that plied the waters, to the Chinese, Indian and Arab communities, to the British colonials in their carriages and horses. In the distance is Government Hill (later known as Fort Canning) with the Governor's Residence, and a row of monumental buildings including the Court House (to the extreme left), the Armenian Church and St Andrew's Church (the two last buildings at right).

In the 1860s, the premises of the newly established Singapore Cricket Club were sited on the western flank of the field, followed by those of the Singapore Recreation Club on the eastern flank in 1884. Both clubs, whose premises sit on the Padang to this very day, cemented the Esplanade's identity and primary function as the premier cricket and sporting grounds in Singapore.

The monumental, administrative appearance of the Esplanade — the Padang as it looks today — only came about from the 1930s, with the construction of the Municipal Offices in 1929 and the Supreme Court in 1939. Both were designed in a spectacular Neo-Classical style common throughout the cities of British India and the British Far East, trumpeting the might and power of the British Empire.

The Esplanade would remain a central rallying point for important events in the city's history, including the surrender parade of the Japanese to the British forces post World War II, and soon after, the British handover of the colony to the local Singaporean government.

Today's Padang still retains its original purpose, being an open green for cricket, rugby and other sporting activities, as well as a major public event space for special occasions such as Singapore's National Day Parade. The spectacular buildings along its flanks have also been immaculately preserved and restored, adding to the sense of its timeless majesty.

COLLYER QUAY, OR THE "SINGAPORE BUND"

When one mentions the word "Bund", one usually refers to a very specific place — the Shanghai Bund. But there were many other "bunds" in the history of city building in the colonial era, particularly in the cities of the British Empire in the East.

The word "bund" simply means a man-made embankment or quay. Like "maidan", it is a Hindi word that the English have borrowed and ultimately adopted in their language — as in Apollo Bund(er) in Bombay. When it is used to describe the Shanghai Bund, however, what the word refers to is not just the man-made embankment, but also the row of stupendous, monumental buildings that line the waterfront. "Bund", in other words, is a variant of "Esplanade" in that both refer to a kind of waterfront promenade, but where the latter is recreational and green, the former is monumental, commercial and urban.

Almost all the port cities in East Asia had bunds; or rather, the word "bund" was used to describe the commercial waterfronts of port cities in the British Far East. One speaks of the Yokohama and Kobe Bunds, still extant today, albeit with only small, isolated pockets of remaining historic architecture; but there was also the Amoy Bund, the Canton Bund and the Hankow Bund, the latter some twice the length of its Shanghai counterpart and with almost all of its buildings still intact.

RIGHT: View of the Singapore Waterfront with (from left to right) Union Building, HSBC Building, Bank of China Building, and the General Post Office, c. 1950s.

Bunds were also to be found in the cities of Georgetown, Penang, and in Singapore, though they weren't popularly known as such. In Singapore, the historic waterfront at Collyer Quay, with its row of monumental commercial buildings, would have been considered the city's Bund. In form, it was no different than the Shanghai Bund, in that its sweeping views of Renaissance and Neo-Classical edifices would have been the first view of the city any immigrant or visitor to these shores would have seen from the decks of their sailing vessels.

The Singapore Bund began to take its form in the late 1850s, with the construction of the first major pier, Johnston's Pier, and the reclamation of land seaward from Commercial Square (later Raffles Place) to form Collyer Quay — the Bund, or embankment proper.

By the late 1860s, the major shipping and financial companies in Singapore had begun building their headquarters and godowns right on the embankment. Chief amongst these were the first Ocean Building built in 1866, the Union Building in 1924, and the original Hong Kong and Shanghai Bank building built in 1892. All three, with their ornate Neo-Classical style and their decorative turrets, would become visible and iconic landmarks.

The early 1920s brought a new rush of building along the waterfront, with the Alkaff Arcade, Singapore's first indoor shopping centre, built in 1909 in an exuberant Moorish style, and the General Post Office, or GPO (also known as the Fullerton Building) built in 1928 in a grand Neo-Classical style.

By the 1930s, Art Deco had made its way to the east, and in 1932, Clifford Pier, an Art Deco masterpiece, replaced the earlier Johnston's Pier

RIGHT TOP: View along Collyer Quay with Alkaff Arcade, early 20th century.

BOTTOM RIGHT: Bank of China Building, c. 1940s.

to become the main port of entry to Singapore for arriving visitors. Post World War II, the Pier was followed by two other Art Deco landmarks in 1954 — the Bank of China Building, and the Asia Insurance Building, then the tallest building in Southeast Asia. Postcard and photographic views of the Bund in the 1950s presented it at its most complete and most iconic.

Commercial imperatives from the 1970s onwards resulted in the unfortunate demolition and replacement of much of the historic architecture on the waterfront. While some of the original commercial institutions, such as the HSBC, the Arcade and Ocean Financial Centre, still stand at the very spot they occupied in the early 1900s, their original Neo-Classical buildings have been replaced by towering skyscrapers of glass and steel.

Thankfully, the Fullerton, Clifford Pier, the Bank of China and the former Asia Insurance Buildings still stand and have been immaculately conserved, providing a glimpse of the Singapore Bund's former glory.

G D COLEMAN AND J T THOMSON,
ARCHITECTS OF MODERN SINGAPORE

In the planning, architecture and urban development of early modern Singapore, two men play a pivotal role: architect George Drumgold Coleman (1796–1844), known more popularly as G D Coleman, and engineer, John Turnbull Thomson (1821–1884).

G D Coleman, an Irishman, was Singapore's pioneer architect in the early colonial period, having planned, designed and built almost anything of significance in the first 15 years of the colony's existence. Arriving after short working stints in Calcutta and Batavia, he had been appointed by Raffles in 1822. One of his first projects was Raffles' Residency on Singapore Hill — which became Government Hill.

In particular, up until the late 1800s, downtown Singapore, or the area east of the Singapore River and to the north of the Esplanade, was an outdoor showcase of the many civic and residential buildings Coleman had designed. Most were in a Palladian style that he had brought over from British India (specifically Calcutta). These included the first Court House, also the very first building in Singapore; the Armenian Church, the first church in Singapore; the first version of St Andrew's Cathedral (called St Andrew's Church then); the original Raffles Institution; and almost all the private residences of some of the colony's wealthiest merchants and European colonials. In John Turnbull Thomson's painting of *The Esplanade from Scandal Point*, all the buildings depicted were designed by Coleman.

In 1833, Coleman was appointed the first Government Superintendent of Public Works, which also made him Superintendent of Convicts. In that

RIGHT: The Courthouse, 1863–1873.

RIGHT: The cupolas at Fort Canning Hill.

position, and employing convicts, he would supervise the construction of Singapore's early road system, notably North and South Bridge Road. He was involved in land reclamation works and land surveys, and published the first comprehensive map of the town of Singapore and its environs in 1836.

Tragically, he died of a tropical fever in Singapore in 1844 (at only 49 years of age), and he was buried in the Christian cemetery at Fort Canning Hill. The headstone from his tomb still exists today and has been placed in the original boundary wall of the cemetery (exhumed in the 1970s). Nearby are two Victorian cupolas he had designed, which stand as elegiac monuments to his life's work.

In the meantime, the handful of his buildings that still stand today, including the first Court House (which survives to this day as part of the Old Parliament House at Empress Place), the Armenian Church and Caldwell House (part of the Convent of the Holy Infant Jesus complex) have been gazetted as National Monuments and are immaculately preserved. The street where he used to live was also named in his honour and a small plaque commemorating him stands on this same street.

John Turnbull Thomson arrived in Malaya in 1838, about a decade after Coleman. He was an engineer and land surveyor, and he began his career surveying and mapping the jungles and the large British estates in the Malayan Peninsula. In 1841, at 21 years of age, he was appointed by the East India Company as the Government Surveyor for the Straits Settlements, and he took up his position in the capital of the Settlements, Singapore.

Here, he continued his work conducting comprehensive topographical, urban and maritime surveys of Singapore and the Singapore Straits, with his first map of Singapore town appearing in 1843, and a subsequent fuller map of Singapore island and the Straits of Singapore appearing in 1844.

In that same year, Thomson succeeded Coleman, in the wake of the latter's passing, as Government Superintendent of Roads and Public Works. In his new position, he oversaw the construction of major landmarks in the city, including the Dalhousie Obelisk (which he designed) at Empress Place, Thomson Road (which is named after him), and Kallang Bridge.

He also designed and built a number of civic and religious buildings, including the European Seamen's Hospital (1845, part of the Singapore General Hospital today), the Chinese Pauper's Hospital (1844, today's Tan Tock Seng Hospital), a tower and spire to St Andrew's Church, as well as the Horsburgh Lighthouse (1851) on Pedra Branca, widely considered to be his crowning achievement.

Thomson was, furthermore, a self-trained but talented artist and in his free time, he sketched and painted panoramas, landscapes and cityscapes of Singapore, Penang, Malacca and Peninsular Malaya. Some of the most memorable of these include his *View of Singapore from Government Hill* from 1846, and his painting of *The Esplanade from Scandal Point*, completed in 1851. These, and the rest of his artistic works, provide a very important window into architecture and life in Singapore and the Straits Settlements.

Thomson eventually left Singapore in the mid 1850s and emigrated to New Zealand soon after. There, he would work his way up to be the colony's first Government Surveyor in 1876, surveying land, drafting maps, designing buildings and painting pictures as he had done in Singapore. He never returned to Singapore again, dying in New Zealand in 1884, aged 63.

RIGHT: Horsburgh Lighthouse on Pedra Branca by John Turnbull Thomson. Paint on paper. 1851.

CHAPTER TWO

MONUMENTS & ARCHITECTURE

MONUMENTS AT EMPRESS PLACE

On the north bank of the Singapore River sits a cluster of Neo-Classical buildings and monuments that functioned as the centre of government through much of Singapore's history. The precinct in which these buildings sit is known as Empress Place, after the public square at the heart of the precinct. This square was in turn accorded the name in 1907, in memory of the late Queen Victoria, Empress of India — hence the name "Empress" — who passed away in 1901.

Neo-Classicism as an architectural movement emerged in the 1800s in Europe, buoyed by the desire on the part of artists, architects, city planners and interior designers to return to a simpler, rational aesthetic epitomised by classical Roman and Greek architecture. It was a very popular architectural form in the colonies, being symbolic of an imposition of rational, Western civilisation upon primordial, heathen cultures — so went the thinking. The British regarded the Neo-Classical (and Palladian, a more specific form of Neo-Classicism), as *the* appropriate architectural style for the Imperial effort, so it appears in all of its major Imperial cities — Calcutta, Bombay, Shanghai, Hong Kong and, naturally, Singapore.

Calcutta, in particular, would be the reference point for Neo-Classical architecture in Singapore in the early to mid 1800s, particularly since, for a period of Singapore's history (1836–1837), the Straits Settlements (Singapore, Penang and Malacca) were administered directly from Calcutta as a Residency (sort of a subdivision) of the Bengal Presidency.

The oldest structure in Empress Place, and quite possibly the oldest surviving building in Singapore, is what is known today as Old Parliament House. This venerable building was originally a two-storey private residence built for Scottish merchant, John Argyle Maxwell, in 1827. Designed by G D Coleman, Maxwell House (as the residence was known) was never once used as a house as Mr Maxwell's businesses were primarily in Java rather than in Singapore and he never took up residence.

Instead, the house was rented by the colonial administration and used as the Courthouse and subsequently Government Offices for much of Singapore's colonial era, becoming the seat of its Legislative Assembly (1955–65), and later on, the House of Parliament when the territory became an independent republic in 1965.

OPPOSITE: The Raffles Library and Museum, early 20th century.

ABOVE: View towards Empress Place and Victoria Memorial Hall, c. 1930s.

BELOW: Close-up of plaque, Dalhousie Obelisk.

Coleman's original design for the building was Palladian, a style that was influenced by the Renaissance-era Italian architect Andrea Palladio. Characteristics included symmetry in layout, the use of pedimented porticos in building façades such that these evoked classical Greco-Roman temples, and the so-called Palladian window — a central arched opening flanked on either side by smaller, rectangular ones and framed with columns.

In the course of successive renovations and improvements during the 1800s, today's Old Parliament House presents a rather more Neo-Classical style of architecture, complete with Corinthian columns. But its original Palladian design is alluded to in the columned pediment and sole Palladian window on the building's front façade.

The second oldest structure in Empress Place is the Dalhousie Obelisk, a curious confection of a monument erected in 1851 to commemorate the Singapore visit from 17th to 19th February of the then Governor-General of India, the Marquis of Dalhousie, James Broun-Ramsay (1812–1860; governorship from 1848–1856). At the time, the Straits Settlements being administered as part of the Bengal Presidency, a visit by the Governor-General of all of British India was quite the major event. All of society, including the leaders of the various ethnic merchant communities in Singapore, turned up.

Designed by John Turnbull Thomson, the obelisk was the first public monument in Singapore, having been funded and erected by a committee of said community leaders, concerned that Singapore would be overlooked in terms of economic investment, and keen to convince the Marquis during his visit that Singapore had great economic potential indeed.

Their efforts to convince the Marquis met with success. Inscriptions on the obelisk, written in English, Jawi, Chinese and Tamil, note that the Marquis had:

> *"emphatically recognised the wisdom of liberating commerce from all restraints under which enlightened policy this Settlement [ie Singapore] has rapidly attained its present rank among British Possessions and with which its future prosperity must ever be identified."*

South of the Obelisk sits Empress Place Building, known formerly as Government Offices, and first completed in 1867. Designed by municipal engineer, Major John Frederick Adolphus (F A) McNair, it housed almost the entire colonial administration at the time, including the Secretariat, the Public Works and the Medical Departments, the Treasury and the Stamp Office, amongst others.

After the public square in front of the Government Offices was renamed Empress Place in 1907, the Offices began to be known first informally and then formally as "Empress Place Building". Post-independence, Empress Place Building continued to host a range of government offices and departments until the late 1990s, when it was repurposed as an exhibition space. In 2003, after a major restoration and renovation, the Asian Civilisations Museum — a museum of Asian art and antiquities — opened its doors in the building.

The architecture of the building is essentially Neo-Classical and it has retained many of its original architectural features, including arcaded verandas, rusticated entrance archways and Doric columns.

The final monument at Empress Place is Victoria Theatre and Concert Hall, actually two separate buildings joined at the hip. Victoria Theatre

RIGHT: Government Offices, early 20th century.

began its life as the city's Town Hall. Designed by municipal engineer, John Bennett, it was completed in 1862 as a two-storey building housing municipal offices on the first floor and a social hall on the second floor.

Victoria Concert Hall was formerly Victoria Memorial Hall, completed in 1905 in the memory of Queen Victoria's passing. It was designed by Regent Alfred John (A J) Bidwell of the architectural firm, Swan & Maclaren. Both buildings are joined by a clock tower, also completed in 1905.

In 1909, Bidwell would be re-employed to remodel the existing Town Hall into a proper public theatre aligned in architectural style to the Memorial Hall. This theatre was renamed Victoria Theatre. Ten years later in 1919, a black statue of Sir Stamford Raffles, created by sculptor Thomas Woolner in 1887 and previously standing in the Esplanade (today's Padang), was moved to the landscaped forecourt of the Victoria Theatre and Memorial Hall, to commemorate the centenary of Singapore's founding.

The architecture of both buildings is a mix of Neo-Classical and Palladian. Considered as a single structure, the Palladian becomes evident in the symmetry of the façade, as well as the use of twin pediments — one on each of the buildings — supported by a row of Corinthian columns. To commemorate Queen Victoria, cartouches bearing the monogram V R I (Victoria Regina Imperatrix or "Victoria, Queen and Empress") may be found on the exterior of the building, emphasising once again the commemorative nature of Empress Place in general.

For much of the 1990s and into the present, Empress Place, including every one of its monuments, has been in the throes of a massive refurbishment project aimed at restoring the precinct to its original early 1900s splendour. In the course of the mid to late 1900s, the precinct was altered dramatically due to vehicular roads being cut through what had initially been public and civic spaces. The public nature of the precinct has been restored through pedestrianisation of roads and the reintroduction of a vast green lawn that used to sit in the forecourt of the Victoria Theatre and Concert Hall. All the former government buildings were gazetted as National Monuments in 1992 and have been repurposed as major cultural venues in the city today.

Ironically, while the original black statue of Stamford Raffles still stands today at the forecourt of the Victoria Theatre and Concert Hall, it is another *white* statue of Raffles, commissioned by the Singapore Tourism Board in 1972 to mark his supposed landing site on the Singapore River, that has become the most visited landmark in this precinct of monuments.

TOP: Victoria Memorial
Hall, early 20th century.

BOTTOM: St Andrew's
Cathedral and the Raffles
Statue, c. 1900s.

St Andrew's Cathedral

St Andrew's Cathedral is the largest and the oldest Anglican Church in Singapore, and the second church to be built in the city (the first being the Armenian Church). It is located just north of the Esplanade (today's Padang), on a site Sir Stamford Raffles himself marked out in his Town Plan, and on land donated by a wealthy Arab merchant, Syed Sharif Omar bin Ali Aljunied.

There were two versions of the Cathedral: the first, known simply as St Andrew's Church, was completed in 1836 to a design by G D Coleman in his typical Palladian style. The Church was dedicated to St Andrew, a patron saint of the Scots, because much of the initial funding for its construction came from the local Scottish community.

In 1842, Coleman's successor, John Turnbull Thomson, erected a tower and spire on Coleman's church building. This enhanced St Andrew's Church can be seen at the far right side of Thomson's famous painting of *The Esplanade from Scandal Point*. Unfortunately, the tower and spire would prove to be short-lived, as they were struck twice by lightning in 1845 and 1849 and deemed unsafe thereafter. By 1852, the entire church building had to be shut due it being structurally unsound. Shortly after, it was demolished.

The second church of St Andrew's was completed in 1864, in an English Neo-Gothic style, with soaring spires, pointed arches and ribbed vaults. It features a large porte-cochère or sheltered carriage porch at its entrance, allowing for members of the congregation to be dropped off in horse carriages right at the church's entrance, sheltered from the heat and the rain.

Designed by civil and mechanical engineer Lieutenant-Colonel Ronald MacPherson, also Superintendant of Convicts, the church featured the use of Madras chunam or chunam plaster, a uniquely British Indian material (and innovation) made from mixing shell lime, egg white, coarse sugar and water with steeped coconut husks. After drying, plastered surfaces would be dusted with fine soapstone powder and polished with rock crystal, resulting in a hard, impenetrable surface and a white exterior.

In style, St Andrew's Church recalled and resembled other magnificent Neo-Gothic cathedrals in British India, chiefly St Paul's Cathedral, built in 1847, in Calcutta and San Thome Basilica, built in 1896, in Mylapore, Madras (today's Chennai). Notably, the church was one of the last buildings in Singapore to be built with Indian convict labour.

St Andrew's Church was upgraded to a Cathedral in 1869 as its congregation continued to grow. In 1973, St Andrew's Cathedral was gazetted as a National Monument, and it continues to serve a very lively, multi-lingual, multi-ethnic congregation today.

OPPOSITE: St Andrew's Cathedral, late 19th century to early 20th century.

A RAFFLES TRINITY

Along Bras Basah Road for much of the late 1800s to the late 1900s sat three of Singapore's most elegant and definitive colonial Neo-Classical monuments, all of which had been named in memory of Sir Stamford Raffles.

The Raffles Institution, the oldest of the three, was founded in 1823 by Raffles himself, as a European-style school dedicated to educating the sons of the various local community leaders. Due to challenges in securing funding, it took the better part of 15 years to construct the school's campus, and it finally opened to students in 1839.

The campus was located on a site bounded by Bras Basah Road, Victoria Road, Stamford Road and Beach Road. Instead of a college, as Raffles had initially envisioned, it opened as the Singapore Institution, an elementary school for young boys. But, between 1844 and 1923, it would transition from an elementary into a secondary school, add a Girl's School, and gradually build new wings to its Bras Basah Campus. In 1868, its name was changed to Raffles Institution, in memory of its founder.

The original Bras Basah Wing of the campus, its most iconic structure, was designed by G D Coleman in his trademark Palladian style. Occupying an entire block along Beach Road, it was a landmark in the city with its series of Palladian façades — pediments, columns and rusticated archways — on both sides of the wing, facing the road and the school's field.

Across Bras Basah Road, literally, from Raffles Institution sat the fabled Raffles Hotel, the *grande dame* of the Far East. Established in 1887 by Armenian hoteliers, the Sarkies Brothers, it first occupied a beach-facing private residence. Within a few years, the hotel would add to its occupancy through a series of expansions, in particular the introduction of its iconic Main Building in 1899.

BELOW: Raffles Institution, late 19th century.

ABOVE AND RIGHT:
Raffles Hotel and
luggage label, early
20th century.

Singapore, Raffles Hotel.

The main building was designed in an exuberant Renaissance Revival style with elements of Palladianism — a Palladian "temple" façade and Palladian windows — and a mix of Doric and Corinthian columns. The entire composition was designed to evoke "grandness", luxury and exclusivity, and takes reference from palace and chateaux architecture in Europe. The architect of the hotel was Regent A J Bidwell of Swan & Maclaren — a name we will see recurring repeatedly in this section of the book.

When Raffles Hotel opened, it was one of the most modern buildings anywhere in the world. Designed with architectural features adapted to the tropics such as high ceilings and large verandas that kept the interior cool and well ventilated, it also boasted mod-cons in the form of electric lights, telephones, call bells and ceiling fans. Its famous Dining Room, with a forest of pillars and a white Carrara marble floor, seated up to 500 people, many of whom were disgorged from large cruise liners docking in Singapore en route to elsewhere in the Far East.

Raffles Hotel was known for its rarefied guest list, which included royalty, heads of state, celebrities, writers and socialites. Some of the more famous of these were Rudyard Kipling, Somerset Maugham and Charlie Chaplin. In the 1950s and '60s, the Hotel became famous for its Long Bar and the Singapore Sling — a local variation of the colonial gin sling — concocted by a Hainanese bartender at the Bar.

Finally, just down the street from Raffles Institution and Raffles Hotel sat the Raffles Library and Museum. Raffles had first mooted the idea of a museum in 1823, and for much of its early history, except for a brief period at Town Hall (the earlier incarnation of Victoria Theatre), both museum and library had been housed within the campus of the Raffles Institution at Bras Basah.

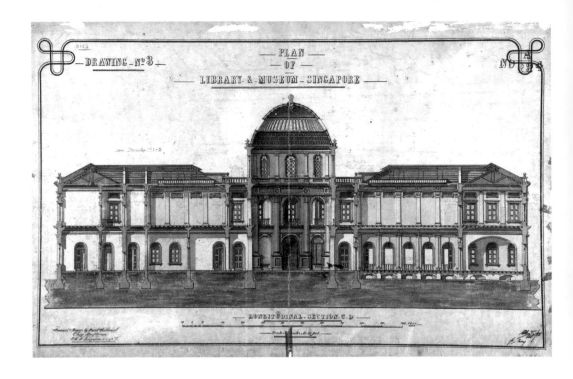

ABOVE: Plans for Raffles Library and Museum, measured and drawn by David Nathaniel, Chief Draftsman, P W D, Singapore, 3.1.1893.

In 1887, a purpose-built building was completed for the Raffles Library and Museum. It was opened on 12 October 1887, by then Governor of the Straits Settlements, Sir Frederick Weld (1812–1860; governorship from 1848–1856). Designed by Engineer, Sir Henry E McCallum, the Main Building of the Library and Museum is yet another Palladian structure — perhaps its most exuberant expression in Singapore — with a central porte-cochère flanked by two Palladian façades with large triangular pediments. Each of these pediments is adorned with the Lion and the Unicorn, the coat of arms of Queen Victoria, and also those of the United Kingdom.

The most significant feature of the library and museum building was its rotunda, capped with a Neo-Classical dome clad with thousands of fish-scaled tiles. On a bright sunny day, the dome would have gleamed, making for a splendid sight from all around the city centre.

Only two of the buildings in the trinity remain today. In 1972, the Raffles Institution, crumbling and decrepit by the mid-1960s, was demolished to make way for a modern mall complex known as Raffles City. Raffles Hotel and the Raffles Library and Museum were, thankfully, gazetted as National Monuments in 1987 and 1992 respectively.

Raffles Hotel, having survived the Great Depression, World War II and Singapore's independence, underwent a major restoration and refurbishment in 1987 that endowed the hotel with modern amenities as well as a shopping arcade in the same Renaissance Revival style. Opened in 1991 to great fanfare, it would go on to spur the restorations of many other grand hotels in the Southeast Asian region.

Meanwhile, the Raffles Library and Museum became the National Museum in 1960 after Singapore attained self-government and after the library moved to its own purpose-built premises (now demolished) right beside the museum. In the 1970s, it changed direction from being primarily a natural history and ethnology museum, relinquished its natural history collections and became primarily a history museum. After a major renovation in the early 2000s, it was restored to its original splendour, re-opening as the National Museum of Singapore in 2006.

THE FULLERTON BUILDING

The Fullerton Building was one of the most important landmarks on the Singapore Waterfront. Located at the mouth of the Singapore River, it replaced the former Fort Fullerton, which existed between 1825 and 1865 and served to protect the colony from a maritime attack; and the former Exchange Building, which stood between 1879 and 1923, and briefly hosted the Post Office.

In 1922, planning began for a new General Post Office building on the site of the Exchange Building. Designed by Major Percy Hubert Keys and his assistant, Frank Dowdeswell — both would later form the Shanghai-based architectural firm Keys and Dowdeswell — the new building opened in 1928 and was christened the "Fullerton Building" after Sir Robert Fullerton (1773–1831), the first Governor of the Straits Settlements from 1826 to 1830, and in acknowledgement of the former Fort Fullerton site.

For much of its history, the building was home to a variety of Government and civic institutions, including the Singapore Club, the Chamber of

RIGHT: The former General Post Office on the Singapore Waterfront. Mid 20th century.

Commerce and the Marine Office. But it would be best known to the local public as the General Post Office or, in more familiar fashion, the "GPO". For much of the 1800s up until the mid 1900s, the basement and ground floor of the building housed the GPO proper, and its various spaces hosted postal halls, sorting rooms and offices.

Post-independence, the building continued to play host to the GPO and a variety of government offices, including the Treasury, Tax Offices and Offices of Economic Development. The GPO itself only moved out of the building in 1996, after which it was extensively refurbished and repurposed into a five-star luxury hotel, aptly named the Fullerton Hotel. The hotel opened in 2001 and in 2015 the building was gazetted as a National Monument.

Architecturally, the building is a fine example of the late Neo-Classical style that was used throughout the British Empire in the 1920s and '30s. Made of reinforced concrete, an innovation in building material at the time, it boasted five exterior-facing façades with monumental two-storey Doric colonnades on each of them. The exterior of the building is adorned with Greco-Roman sculptures created by Swiss sculptor Rudolf Wening and Italian sculptor Cavaliere Rudolfo Nolli (1888–1963, "Cavaliere" is the Italian equivalent of a Knighthood, ie "Sir").

Inside, the building boasted state-of-the-art facilities like lifts, automated mail sorting equipment, a 300-foot long postal counter and a tunnel that ran underground from the building to the pier, allowing for smooth and efficient delivery of mail from steamships arriving at the harbour.

The monumental nature of the Fullerton Building recalls the British tradition of constructing palatial (ie inspired by palaces) and elaborate General Post Offices in British India and the Straits Settlements: the GPOs in the major Imperial metropolises of Calcutta, Bombay, Madras and Penang, all of which still stand today, provide examples. The intent of such palatial monumentalism as applied to an ostensibly civic space such as a post office was undoubtedly to underscore the power and legitimacy of the British Imperial effort and to discourage any second-guessing as to their right to rule.

THE SUPREME COURT AND CITY HALL BUILDINGS

Along the north flank of the Padang today sit two majestic civic buildings in grand Neo-Classical style, built in the Inter-War period. These were the largest buildings of Singapore's colonial era, and their very location on the former Esplanade, and their majestic imposing nature speaks to the power and the might of the British Empire at the time. For much of the mid 1900s, the two buildings could be seen by sea-going vessels arriving in Singapore harbour, and they would have presented an awe-inspiring sight.

ABOVE: Supreme Court and Municipal Offices, early 20th century.

BELOW: Close-up of the rotunda, former Supreme Court.

The older building of the two is the former City Hall, completed in 1929. It replaced a row of private residences designed and built by G D Coleman and which can be seen in John Turnbull Thomson's painting of *The Esplanade from Scandal Point*. Originally called the Municipal Building, it housed the Municipal Council of Singapore, which was responsible for maintaining public infrastructure, and for providing water, electricity and gas to the city. It was formally renamed "City Hall" only in 1951, when King George VI conferred "city" status on Singapore.

Over the decades, City Hall has provided a backdrop to many significant milestones in Singapore history. This was where Lord Louis Mountbatten (1900–1979) accepted the surrender of the Japanese forces in 1945; where the first Prime Minister of Singapore, Lee Kuan Yew (1923–2015), was sworn in in 1959; and where the latter would read the Proclamation of Malaysia in 1963, ending colonial rule. After independence in 1965, City Hall remained the venue for the swearing in of senior Members of Parliament.

The building was designed by municipal architects F D Meadows and Alexander Gordon, who, realising full well the strategic location of the building, created a façade that was self-consciously Imperial, recalling temples and palaces of ancient Rome and Greece. In style, the building combined aspects of both Neo-Classical and emergent Modernist architecture, which called for simplicity and functionality in form, a reduction of ornamentation, innovation in structure and the use of new, industrially produced materials.

The façade was quintessentially Neo-Classical, with its colonnade of colossal Corinthian columns, and the grand stairway leading up to its main entrance. The columns and stone cladding had been designed and built by an Italian sculptor and architect, Cavaliere Rudolfo Nolli, who had also adorned the façade of the nearby Fullerton Building.

The monumental nature of the building (it extended some 370 feet in length along the Padang), its blocky rectangular shape with flat roof and its sombre, gray granite cladding, was essentially Modernist. The design of the interior also eschewed excessive ornamentation for a stark and functional aesthetic.

The former Supreme Court building was completed a decade later in 1939, and was a whole-hearted return to lavish and heavily ornamented Neo-Classicism. Designed by Chief Architect of the Public Works Department, Frank D Ward, it occupied the exact location of the former Grand Hotel de L'Europe — one of the finest hotels in Singapore, on a par with the Raffles Hotel at the turn of the 19th century, though shut and demolished due to financial difficulties by the early 1930s.

The Supreme Court was the very last Neo-Classical building to be built in Singapore and heralded the passing of an era. Like City Hall, it presents an impressive façade of enormous Corinthian columns. But the resemblance ends there. The central façade of the building harks back to the Palladian style popular in the mid to late 1800s, with its immense pediment straddling six columns. Within the tympanum of the pediment is a sculpture, also undersigned by Cavaliere Rudolfo Nolli, depicting the Allegory of Justice. Topping the entire edifice is a stupendous rotunda and copper dome that recalls the dome of St Paul's Cathedral in London.

Inside, innovations in design and materials prevail. Chinese craftsman fleeing to Singapore on account of the Sino-Japanese War brought with them new and superior techniques of plaster finishing that had been used to great effect in Shanghai. Efforts to keep costs low meant marble was avoided and instead Art Deco rubber tiles made to resemble marble tiles were used for flooring.

In 1992, City Hall and the Supreme Court were gazetted as National Monuments. Both buildings would retain their original functions until 2005, when an announcement was made by the Government to repurpose and link them together as a National Gallery of Art. Following a decade of planning, design, restoration and refurbishment, National Gallery Singapore opened to great fanfare in late 2015, affording a new lease of life to the two grandest colonial monuments in Singapore.

SWAN & MACLAREN — ARCHITECTS OF MODERN SINGAPORE

No other architectural firm has had as large an impact on the architecture of modern Singapore as Swan & Maclaren. The list of buildings in Singapore that they have either designed and built, or restored and improved, is staggering and includes over a dozen of today's National Monuments, as well as many other landmarks that have featured prominently in Singapore's

commercial and religious history. The history of Swan & Maclaren, still in
business today after more than 100 years, is the history of Singapore itself.

The firm's defining feature may be its ability to adapt itself to the times;
and its mastery, therefore, of a surprising variety of architectural styles both
Western and Eastern. Over the years, its various architects have dabbled in
Neo-Classical, Edwardian and Renaissance Revival architecture (in the late
1800s and early 1900s), Modernist and Eclectic East-West styles (in the mid
1900s) and startlingly contemporary vernaculars (today).

The firm was originally called Swan & Lermit, formed in 1887 by two
engineers and land surveyors, the Messrs Archibald Swan and Alfred Lermit.
In 1890, Lermit left the firm and was replaced by a James Waddell Boyd
Maclaren; and so the firm took on the name "Swan & Maclaren" in 1892.

The single most important architect in the firm was neither Swan nor
Maclaren, however, but a gentleman by the name of Regent Alfred John
Bidwell (1869–1918), or R A J Bidwell for short. Unlike Swan or Maclaren,
Bidwell was a professionally trained architect, only the second of such to
arrive in Singapore after G D Coleman. He joined the firm in 1897, and
because of his eye for beauty, symmetry and proportion, as well his vast
architectural range, he won commissions for many of the most important
buildings at the turn of the 19th century.

The list of buildings undersigned by Bidwell, demonstrating his vast
architectural range, included commercial properties such as the Raffles Hotel
Main Building (1899) in a spectacular Renaissance Revival and Palladian
style; the Oranje Building (1904), today's Stamford House, in a Venetian
Renaissance Style; the former Malaysian Publishing House, or MPH

RIGHT: Majestic Theatre (left) and the Great Southern Hotel (right), c. 1950s. Both buildings were designed by Swan & Maclaren.

Building (1908) in an Edwardian style; and John Little's Department Store at Raffles Place (1907, demolished), in an Ibero-Moorish style.

He also undersigned some spectacular civic and religious buildings, including the Victoria Memorial Hall (1905) in a Neo-Classical style; the former Teutonia Club, later renamed the Goodwood Park Hotel (1900), in an eye-catching German Rhineland vernacular, and the Chesed-El Synagogue at Oxley Rise (1905) in Late Renaissance Style.

In addition to all these achievements, Bidwell is also credited with the invention of the colonial "black-and-white" house in Singapore at the turn of 19th century, having designed some of the earliest exemplars of this hybrid form, which combined a Tudor Revival Style with local Malay adaptations for tropical weather.

Bidwell left the firm in 1911, but Swan & Maclaren continued to land prestigious commissions from government and financial institutions as well as wealthy local magnates such as Eu Tong Sen and Tan Kah Kee. Some of its most iconic works in the early 20th century include the Eu Villa (1912, demolished), the private villa of Chinese magnate Eu Tong Sen; the original Ocean Building (1923, demolished); the Hong Kong Bank Chambers (1925, demolished) on the Singapore waterfront; and the Chinese High School Campus (1925) at Bukit Timah.

It was during the Inter-War years (1920s–1930s), also, that the firm began to design in a very self-conscious Eclectic style, drawing from a larger movement of hybrid East-West architecture that was also emerging in the Asian region. The basic building blocks of the Eclectic consisted of a European-style building foundation that was finished with Asian-style ornamentation, adornments and roof forms.

Some fine examples of this style include the Sultan Mosque in Kampong Glam, rebuilt in 1929 in a resplendent Indo-Saracenic style imported from

British India; the Telok Ayer Methodist Church (1925) on Amoy Street with its Chinese-style roof and Byzantine-style ornamentation; and the Majestic Theatre first built as a Cantonese Opera theatre (1928) and known for its exuberant mosaic-tiled façade, a Chinese take on Art Deco. Another significant landmark from this period is the Tanjong Pagar Railway Station (1931) in spectacular Art Deco.

Post-War and post-Independence, the firm continued on its tried and tested path of taking commissions for a range of different types of buildings, from hospitals to commercial properties to civic monuments, experimenting with Art Deco, Modernist and later more contemporary architectural styles. It has, however, not had the same impact on Singapore's contemporary skyline and architectural scene as it did in the early 1900s, when the firm was at the top of its game.

RAFFLES PLACE — THE ARCHITECTURE OF COMMERCE

Raffles Place began as Commercial Square in 1823, a business and trading centre in the new colony of Singapore, reclaimed from swampy land on the south bank of the Singapore River. Originally, it was a park and green space measuring some 200 yards by 50 yards. But, eventually, with the rapid development of the colony, the park began to be flanked by numerous international trading houses and financial institutions. It was renamed Raffles Place in 1858, in honour of the colony's founder.

BELOW: View of Raffles Place, looking towards the Chartered Bank of India, China and Australia, c. 1930s.

RIGHT TOP: Façade of John Little, c. 1900s.

RIGHT BELOW: China Building on Chulia Street, built in 1929, was the headquarters of the Oversea-Chinese Banking Corporation (OCBC).

Then, as now, the square was the commercial heart of the city, playing host to the local headquarters of major international banks, merchant houses, as well as the island's largest department stores. As the colony grew in stature and wealth, the edifices flanking the square become grander and more ostentatious. Views of Raffles Place from the early 1900s depict a bustling square that would not have looked out of place in London or New York; it was surrounded on all four sides by elegant European buildings in the latest architectural styles, chiefly Renaissance Revival, Neo-Classical and Palladian architecture — the architecture of trade and commerce in the colonies.

The headquarters of the Chartered Bank of India, Australia and China (the forerunner of today's Standard Chartered Bank) stood at the eastern end of Raffles Place, along Bonham Street. It was completed in 1915 in a

ABOVE: Advertisement for Robinsons & Co., c. 1900s.

Neo-Classical style with Doric columns, and a spectacular dome. It was one of the defining landmarks of Raffles Place, dominating many postcard views of the city in the 1930s to the 1950s. Unfortunately, it was demolished in 1981 and replaced with today's Standard Chartered Bank building.

Immediately to the left of the Chartered Bank was the Renaissance Revival style Bonham Building, at the corner of Chulia Street and Bonham Street. This was where the United Chinese Bank (later renamed the United Overseas Bank) operated, from its establishment in 1935. The building was demolished in the early 1970s and replaced with the present UOB Plaza Two.

To the right of the Chartered Bank building stood the premises of one of the oldest commercial establishments in Raffles Place, the former John Little & Co department store, built in 1907 by architectural firm Swan & Maclaren in an exuberant Ibero-Moorish Renaissance style. John Little was founded 1842 and up until 2016, when it finally shut its doors, was the oldest retail store in Singapore still in business. Its department store premises in Raffles Place would be demolished in 1973 to make way for offices.

Diagonally across from John Little's sat its competitor, Robinson & Co., also one of the oldest department stores in Singapore, having been founded in 1858. It occupied the Raffles Chambers building, a stately Palladian structure with an iconic statue of Eros on the roof. For much of the 1930s till the 1970s, it was one of the most popular department stores in the city. Unfortunately, the building was destroyed by fire in 1972, but unlike John Little, the store continues to operate today along Orchard Road.

Beside Robinson's stood the Neo-Classical Meyer Chambers building, built in 1930 by Swan & Maclaren. It housed the headquarters of the Overseas Union Bank from 1949 (and was later renamed OUB Chambers). Demolished in the 1970s, the site of the building, and the adjacent plot where Robinson's formerly sat, would become home to the headquarters of the OUB Centre at 1 Raffles Place, opened in 1986.

Finally, at the western end of Raffles Place, stood the headquarters of the Chartered Mercantile Bank of India and China, built in Neo-Classical style. It was the last historic building standing on Raffles Place, demolished in 1984 to make way for the construction of the Raffles Place Mass Rapid Transit Station.

Today's Raffles Place would be totally unrecognisable to a tourist from the 1930s returning to visit the city. That said, Raffles Place continues to be the best place in the city to admire the architecture of trade and commerce, except, of course, today's architecture consists of decidedly towering skyscrapers in glass, steel and concrete.

The Advent of Art Deco

Art Deco as an architectural form emerged in France just before World War I and became a major international phenomenon and defining architectural style of the 1920s and 1930s. The word "Art Deco" comes from the French *Arts Decoratifs et Industriels Modernes*, or "Modern Decorative and Industrial Arts". It was a self-consciously modern style of the time, heavily inspired by industrialisation, new technologies and building materials, and the anticipation of the advent of a "Machine Age". This über-modernity also gave it an air of exclusivity and it became associated with luxury, wealth, decadence and, in particular, moving pictures and the entertainment industry.

Defining features of Art Deco primarily include the use of geometric and symmetrical forms over organic ones — forms that allude to and may only be produced by machines rather than humans. In a nod, however, to traditions of craft and architecture, these geometric forms are often then adorned with lavish but stylised figural representations and painted in bright colours.

From France, Art Deco spread to Europe and America, and onwards to the colonies of the East by the late 1920s and '30s. It became tremendously popular in the United States, where it was used for skyscrapers in the major cities of New York, Chicago, San Francisco and Los Angeles, and to great effect in the waterfront city of Miami.

BELOW: Tanjong Pagar Railway Station, c. 1930s.

Elsewhere, Art Deco was also used in the major trading and commercial capitals of the East, particularly in Shanghai which, like New York City, adopted Art Deco as a style for many of its skyscrapers and residential buildings; and also Bombay (Mumbai), which retains one of the largest number of Art Deco buildings, mostly residential, in the world.

In Singapore, Art Deco arrived in the late 1920s, and remained till long after World War II. In particular, it continued to influence the design of skyscrapers in the Financial District until well into the '70s — the I M Pei – designed OCBC Centre, built in 1976, is an example of a Modernist style inspired by Art Deco — and it also informed and changed commercial architectural vernaculars such as the traditional Nanyang shophouse.

Perhaps the most important and striking example of Art Deco in Singapore is Tanjong Pagar Railway Station, designed by Swan & Maclaren and completed in 1931. It was to be the southernmost terminal of the Federated Malay States Railways, with stations along the western coast of Malaya. The façade consists of a blocky cubic template adorned with stylised human figures — allegories for Agriculture, Commerce, Transport and Industry. Interestingly, the roofs of the station are covered with Chinese-style ceramic tiles typically found atop Chinese temples and courtyard houses. The station was gazetted as a National Monument in 2011 and is currently due to be refurbished into a multi-purpose lifestyle and events space.

Of the three major stations along the FMSR route — Kuala Lumpur (completed in 1910), Ipoh (completed in 1917), and Singapore — only the latter was designed in an Art Deco style, as if alluding to Singapore's premier status as the commercial and entertainment centre of British Malaya. Its sister stations were built in an Indo-Saracenic style, with distinctive Mughal elements such as domes and minarets on a European, Neo-Classical base.

LEFT: Interior of Clifford Pier, today's Fullerton Bay Hotel.

Another iconic Art Deco gem in Singapore is Clifford Pier, built in 1933 to replace the earlier Johnston's Pier. Both Clifford and Johnston's Piers, located on the Singapore waterfront, were the primary landing and departure points for visitors and immigrants to Singapore. Generations of visitors would recount stepping off their cruise liners and taking their first steps on the island right here, on the pier off the edge of Raffles Place.

Clifford Pier was designed by Frank Dorrington Ward, Chief Engineer of the Public Works Department. The design of its façade was dramatic but far less ornate than that of Tanjong Pagar Railway station, demonstrating an obvious, gradual shift in the application of Art Deco. The entrance façade consisted of long, stacked panels of concrete shot through the middle with a sunburst-like entrance portal that was sheltered by a large, cast-iron porte-cochère. A coat of arms of the Straits Settlements sits at the top of the entrance façade, and the entire structure itself is topped with a single flagpole.

What is most distinctive about this building, however, is the structure of its roof, consisting of a simple but ingenious system of trussed and over-lapping concrete arches recalling the buttresses of a Gothic cathedral (albeit far more heavy and industrial in look and feel). The vast, semi-cylindrical space that results from this trussed arch structure affords the heavy concrete building an otherwise light, airy and expansive interior.

Clifford Pier was conserved and restored in the late 2000s, opening in 2010 as the entrance foyer to the Fullerton Bay Hotel.

A little more recent is the Cathay Building along Orchard Road, constructed between 1937 and 1941 and designed by British Architect Frank Brewer. When it opened in 1939, it was the tallest building in Singapore and Southeast Asia. A temple to modern leisure and entertainment, it was the headquarters of the British Malaya Broadcasting Corporation, and also housed the historic 1,300-seat Cathay Cinema, the Cathay Hotel and the Cathay Restaurant.

In style, Cathay Building is even more stark and simple than Clifford Pier, progressing along the Art Deco trajectory towards the use of entirely non-organic and non-stylised geometric shapes. This futuristic Art Deco style was used to demonstrate Cathay Building and Cathay Cinema's ultra-modernity in relation to its competitors on Orchard Road, such as the Alhambra Cinema and Capitol Theatre, which had been built in slightly older architectural styles — Neo-Classical for the former, and a transitional style incorporating elements of Art Deco and Neo-Classicism for the latter.

Unfortunately, much of Cathay Building has not survived and only its Art Deco façade, with rounded, stepped walls and large vertical signage spelling "CATHAY" has been preserved. This façade was gazetted as a National Monument in 2003 and still fronts the present Cathay Building, a contemporary, glass-clad building that still houses Cathay Cinema and other leisure establishments.

Tiong Bahru Housing Estate presents a final, rather interesting, instance of Art Deco in Singapore. Begun in 1936, it was the earliest public housing estate in the city, commissioned and built by the Singapore Improvement Trust (SIT), a branch of the colonial government. It was designed by architect Alfred G Church in a Streamline Moderne style. This is a very late variation on the Art Deco movement, inspired by modern travel and

BELOW: Cathay Building, c. 1940s.

transportation. Defining features of this style include decorative elements that recall automobiles, aeroplanes and ocean liners. Streamline Moderne also broke away from "traditional" Art Deco in that it was far less lavishly decorated, opting instead for clean, horizontal lines and a kind of light, sweeping, aerodynamic feel.

Tiong Bahru Housing Estate was built between 1936 and 1941, with some 784 flats, 54 tenements and 33 shops, housing some 6,000 persons at the time. No further development took place again until 1954. The largest of these flats sat at Block 78, Moh Guan Terrace, and it continues to stand today. The Streamline Moderne style is evident in specific features of many of the flats: the use of circular windows recalling cruise-ship portholes and long, horizontal balconies and elongated buildings that recall early aeroplanes are clear.

Twenty of the apartment blocks built between 1936 to 1941 were gazetted for conservation in 2003. Tiong Bahru itself has evolved into a fashionable residential precinct known for its bars, restaurants, boutique cafés, fashion outlets and independent bookshops, and it has become known for its "hipster" and Bohemian vibe.

HYBRID ARCHITECTURES I — THE COLONIAL BLACK-AND-WHITE

In the 1920s and '30s, architectural styles in the colonies of the East began to fuse both European and traditional elements, particularly in the forms of private residential buildings. In the Netherlands East Indies (today's Indonesia), an *Indische* style emerged that fused simple Dutch patrician-style buildings with architectural elements designed to cope with the tropical weather in the Malay Archipelago. In the suburbs of Batavia (today's Jakarta),

Soerabaja and Semarang were to be found hundreds of these *Indische*-style houses with their steep roofs, north-south alignment, large ground-floor verandas and high ceilings.

Elsewhere, in the Philippines, a similar hybrid form called the *bahay na bato* evolved from the fusion of Spanish colonial vernaculars with indigenous Filipino architecture. These townhouses, with large sliding balconies and latticed windows filled with mother of pearl to blot out the sunlight, had ground floors built from stone and upper floors of wood. They were a common sight in the metropolitan cities of Manila and Baguio — and some remain today.

British Malaya and, in particular, Singapore, also evolved its own unique form of hybrid residential architecture, found nowhere else in the world. This is what is known today as the colonial Black-and-White.

In form, the Black-and-White draws reference from the Anglo-Indian bungalow, originating in Bengal (from whence the term "*bangala*" contorted to "bungalow" by the English came). This was most commonly found in the suburbs and cantonments of the cities of British India — Calcutta, Bombay, Madras and Rangoon. These were essentially European cottages transplanted from Britain to India, with architectural features designed to adapt to the Indian sub-tropical weather: large covered verandas to keep out the rain and protect from the sun, high ceilings to ensure air circulation, and tall louvred and shuttered windows to take in the breeze.

When these Anglo-Indian bungalows were imported to Malaya, further innovations took place to take into account the humid, torrid tropical weather. Aspects from the basic form of the local kampong house were incorporated. In particular, local architectural wisdom called for lifting the house off the

RIGHT: Ardmore House, late 19th century. This is an example of tropical plantation-style architecture in Singapore with antecedents in the Anglo-Indian bungalow.

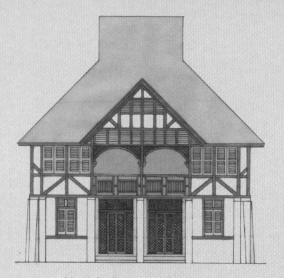

House for Captain Kinghorn, 1904

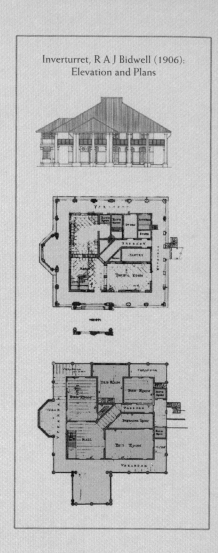

Inverturret, R A J Bidwell (1906):
Elevation and Plans

British American Co., Nassim Road, Swan & Maclaren (1920)

Glen Cree 1897

LEFT: Three drawings of Black-and-White bungalows in Singapore in the Tudor Revival style.

ABOVE: Plans of Inverturret.

ground with plinths, pillars and arches in order to avoid flooding and wild animals. But these hybrid houses — many of them sitting in the midst of vast spice and rubber plantations — were not yet colonial Black-and-Whites.

The Black-and-White style flourished in Singapore for only a brief period of time between the late 1890s and the early 1930s, and then again post World War II when a more military style emerged. The hybrid form of the colonial Black-and-White is rather specific, consisting of elements taken from European Tudor-style houses and those of the Anglo-Indian-Malay Bungalow.

The design of the colonial Black-and-White draws reference from the Tudor Revival or "Tudorbethan" style that emerged in the late 19th century in England. This was a nostalgic throwback to the mediaeval styles of the Elizabethan era (17th century), emphasising timber and traditional methods of building. The upper levels of the colonial Black-and-White were thus built with wood, with exposed timbering on the façade. The intent was to recall Tudor houses in England. Timber elements in the upper floors were typically painted brown or black, in stark contrast with the walls, which were whitewashed, giving rise to the colloquial name "black-and-white".

The lower half of the house was in typical Anglo-Malay bungalow style with the entire house lifted off the ground on sturdy plinths. The bungalow was built with locally sourced materials and with deep consideration for not only the tropical weather, but also the immediate terrain and environment around the house.

Black-and-Whites were the domain of the colonial elite in Singapore, often commissioned and built as private residences by senior civil servants, wealthy shipping or trading magnates, and plantation lords. Many of them sat in the once verdant plantation area of Orchard and Tanglin Roads, which then became the most exclusive private residential districts in Singapore. The single most sought-after architect for these Black-and-Whites was R A J Bidwell of Swan & Maclaren, who designed and erected some of the most stupendous of these edifices at the turn of the 19th century, and is often credited with "inventing" the form.

Unfortunately, being almost always private residences, little of the traditional Black-and-Whites remains today. Most of the 500 or so that still stand and have been conserved by the Urban Redevelopment Authority belong to a later variety of Black-and-White, built to house military officers in exclusively military cantonments (for example, in today's Portsdown Road, Alexandra Park and Admiralty areas). Those that were private residences remain as isolated instances throughout the island, and are clustered in a few precincts such as Nassim Road, Chatsworth Park and Ridout Park.

Perhaps the best still-standing example of a colonial Black-and-White, and also the oldest Black-and-White built in Singapore, is Atbara at 5 Gallop Road, named after a River in Sudan and owned by John Burkinshaw, one of the founders of Donaldson and Burkinshaw, the second oldest law firm in

Singapore. Built in 1898 to a design by Bidwell, it is the earliest exemplar of the Black-and-White style, with its main wooden body lifted off the ground by elegant pillars and Victorian-Moorish arches.

Just beside it is Inverturret, at 7 Gallop Road, built in 1902 and designed also by Bidwell. It has a distinctive porte-cochère, large ground-floor sheltered verandas and tall balconies on the upper floor. It was the residence of Charles MacArthur, one of the earliest chairmen of the Straits Trading Company.

For almost 60 years (1939–1999), both properties housed the French Embassy and the residence of the French Ambassador. At present they have been refurbished as part of the Gallop Extension of the Singapore Botanic Gardens, and transformed into museums dedicated to Singapore's natural history.

Hybrid Architectures II — The Nanyang Shophouse

The other quintessential, and rather more ubiquitous, hybrid architectural form in Singapore is the traditional Nanyang shophouse, known as the Singapore shophouse (though it is admittedly not unique to Singapore).

This hybrid vernacular is a mix of European, Chinese and occasionally Malay architectural elements and is a direct result of centuries of maritime trade between China's east coast port cities, particularly the cities of the Hokkien and Canton provinces, and the Southeast Asian region, which the Chinese called the "Southern Seas" or Nanyang (南洋).

Everywhere there are Southern Chinese communities in Southeast Asia, we find variations on the Nanyang shophouse. They are to be found in the Straits Settlement cities of Malacca, Penang and Singapore, of course, with their majority Chinese communities; but also in the cities of Rangoon, Batavia, Soerabaja, Bangkok, Phuket, Hoi An, Hanoi, Saigon, Phnom Penh and even tiny Vientiane.

Back in the "home country", prototypical shophouse forms can also be found in proliferation in the treaty port cities of Canton (Guangzhou), Amoy (Xiamen), Foochow (Fuzhou) and Swatow (Shantou) — all these being cities from whence the Chinese left in droves to seek fortune and opportunity in the Southern Seas, bringing with them their traditions of craft and architecture.

The Chinese-ness of the traditional shophouse is inherent in its basic form, which is a variation on Chinese courtyard houses typical of Southern China, wherein living quarters encircle a central courtyard. In a similar fashion, all shophouses retain a basic configuration of living quarters surrounding a modest airwell or courtyard space, all of which is crammed within a tight, elongated, rectangular floorplan adapted to city living.

This unique floorplan with its narrow street frontage and long deep interiors is a direct result of street frontage tax, wherein residences and

OPPOSITE TOP: Atbarra, by R A J Bidwell.

OPPOSITE BOTTOM: Inverturret, by R A J Bidwell.

businesses were taxed according to how much street frontage they occupied. This tax system also had its origins in China, and was adopted by the Dutch and the British in their administration of the Straits Settlements city of Malacca. It would prove instrumental in cementing the basic form of the shophouse.

As its name suggests, the shophouse is essentially a mixed commercial and residential structure, with the front section of the ground floor being a commercial store front, and the upper levels and back sections of the ground floor being residential. Later on, purely residential, suburban forms evolved as Chinese communities became more affluent and desired their own exclusive villas away from the bustle of downtown.

To facilitate commerce and provide shelter from the weather, colonial regulations during Raffles' time stipulated that every shophouse provide a sheltered forecourt of a minimum width of five feet. As shophouses were designed to be built in long terraced rows, the resulting architectural feature this regulation precipitated was the "five foot way" — a sheltered pedestrian walkway that allowed for passers-by to promenade, view goods on display, and carry out transactions with shopkeepers. It also protected people, goods and shopfronts from intense heat and torrential rain.

Shophouses were continuously built between the 1840s to the 1960s and demonstrate a surprising diversity of architectural styles from Neo-Classical to Transitional to Art Deco. The façades of the shophouse were where their hybrid nature was most evident, with many blending European ornamental features such as pilasters and columns in the various Classical orders (Doric, Ionic, Corinthian), French windows and fanlights, and Portuguese-style

BELOW LEFT: Peranakan-style tiles.

BELOW RIGHT: Five-foot way, Blair Road.

RIGHT: Shophouses along New Bridge Road, early 20th century.

tiling on walls and floors, with traditional Chinese-style adornment such as the *pintu pagar* (or Chinese-style swinging saloon door), Chinese calligraphy and Chinese flora and fauna motifs. Sheltered verandas and pitched roofs were an adaptation to the tropical, rainy weather with the occasional stepped eaves being an appropriation of a Malay architectural form.

Perhaps the most unique and noteworthy shophouse style is that of the "Chinese Baroque", which emerged in the early decades of the 1900s. It was characterised by an effusive, ostentatious and thoroughly over-the-top use of surface ornamentation that combined the best (or worst, depending on one's point of view) of Classical and Chinese aesthetic style. On the most ornate of these specimens, Corinthian capitals and French casement windows jostle for space alongside elaborate plasterwork, stucco and wood carvings depicting dragons, kirins, phoenixes and scenes from Chinese myth and morality tales. The overall effect is dizzying and surreal.

Thankfully, thousands of shophouses have been conserved and immaculately restored in Singapore, resulting in the shophouse being one of the unique and defining features of the city's urban landscape. Large tracts of commercial shophouses can be found in downtown Singapore, primarily in Chinatown (Tanjong Pagar Road, Neil Road, Duxton Road, Bukit Pasoh and so on), but also in other historic districts of Kampong Glam, Little India, Jalan Besar, Balestier and further afield in the East Coast districts of Katong, Geylang and Joo Chiat.

The most impressive residential shophouses may be found in Emerald Hill. This residential area was almost exclusively the abode of wealthy Baba-Nyonya families and featured houses in the "Chinese Baroque" style. They represent the apogee of the Nanyang-style shophouse, and are a unique contribution to Singapore and World Heritage.

Malay Woman, Singapore.

CHAPTER THREE

CULTURES & COMMUNITIES

THE MALAYS

"Perahu baharu, temberang pun baharu
Baharu sekali masuk Melaka.
Abang baharu, adik pun baharu,
Baharu sekali kenal biasa."

"Both ship and shrouds alike were new,
When first we made Malacca's port;
You, sir, are new, and I am too,
And for the first time we consort."

— Old Malay song, from *Malay Pantuns*,
translated and compiled by A W Hamilton (1932)

O f all the ethnic communities that make up contemporary Singapore, the Malays were the first to arrive.

From across the oceans they came in early antiquity, settling and colonising all the islands of what would be known as the Malay Archipelago. From whence they came remains a mystery. Some academics have them originating in the southern Chinese island of Taiwan, migrating in primitive though sturdy vessels across the islands of the East. Others have them originating in situ, at a time before the Ice Age when large tracts of the archipelago weren't an archipelago at all, but part of a continental shelf known as Sundaland.

While the Malays are primarily Muslim today, they weren't always so. In classical antiquity — the 7th to the 13th centuries — they were variously a Hindu and Buddhist peoples.

Of the many great empires and kingdoms of the pre-Islamic Malays, two in particular stand out. The first is the mighty Srivijaya Empire (7th to 12th century), a maritime power which held sway over much of what is today's Peninsula Malaya, Sumatra and Java. It was a Buddhist empire, with its capital at the fabled Sumatran city of Palembang. Very little archaeologically speaking remains of it today. The best trace of its existence is the magnificent Buddhist monument of Borobudur in East Java, built in the 9th century by the Sailendran Kings of Java, vassals of Srivijaya.

OPPOSITE: Portrait of a Malay Woman, c. 1903.

ABOVE: Wayang Wong
dancer, c. 1900s.

Srivijaya was followed by an even more formidable maritime empire, the Majapahit (13th to early 16th century). This empire of Hindu kings ruled over almost all of what is today's Malaysia and Indonesia from their central base of East Java. They left a plentiful array of archaeological traces of their past — the likes of the Hindu Temples of Prambanan, and the many exquisite Hindu sculptures in the halls of the National Museum of Indonesia.

Then came a significant rupture from the past that would prove pivotal to establishing a Malay cultural identity that endures until today. This was the establishment of the Malacca Sultanate (1411–1511) on the west coast of Peninsula Malaya. The first Sultan of Malacca had fled Singapura in the early 1500s, and upon establishing his new kingdom, converted to Islam (though when *exactly* he converted remains uncertain).

One of the most significant legacies of Malacca was the adoption of Islam as the State religion and its eventual transmission to almost the entire Malay World. Another significant legacy was the codification of laws, ritual and culture, even down to details in dress and language. In other words, the Malacca Sultanate defined what it meant to be Malay.

Malacca would fall to the Portuguese in 1511, and its last Sultan flee to Johor-Riau to establish a new Sultanate there. But the spectre of Malacca would live on. Even today, the many royal houses of Peninsula Malaya claim lineage from Malacca and in their sacred rituals invoke the glory and splendour of the legendary city.

The Malays are not one homogeneous group. In fact, the Malay community in Singapore today — having arrived in the city to trade and seek their fortune in the course of centuries — come from all over Nusantara or the Malay Archipelago. There are the Melayu, of course — the peoples of the Malay Peninsula, the Riau Islands and the Eastern coast of Sumatra. These are the direct descendants of Srivijaya and Malacca. They make up the majority of the Malays in Singapore.

But there are also the Javanese from Java, known for their courtly elegance and their elaborate *keris* and *sarong kebaya*. Likewise, the Bugis, fabled seafarers and traders, who for centuries have plied the waters of Nusantara from their homeland in Sulawesi, formerly known as Celebes. The Minangkabau, from Padang in West Sumatra: a matrilineal peoples famed for their *rumah gadang*, or traditional houses with roofs shaped like the horns of the buffalo; and for their *nasi padang*, a meal of rice with mixed dishes that has become a staple in Singapore.

There are the Bawean (also known as the Boyanese), from the tiny island of Bawean, off Surabaya, who became drivers and horse-trainers. The Banjar, from the southeastern coast of Borneo, who were traders in gemstones; and the Christian Bataks from the highlands of Lake Toba in Sumatra, once believed to have practised ritual cannibalism.

Finally, there are the Orang Laut, or "sea gypsies". They did not consider themselves Malays proper, being of the sky and sea rather than of earth and jungle. They lived their lives entirely on boats and stilt-houses along the coasts of Singapura and Peninsula Malaya and made a living through fishing and other related activities. They were intensely nomadic and were known by various names in Singapore — Orang Kallang, Orang Seletar, Orang Gelam — depending on where they settled.

The cultural heart of the Malay community in Singapore is Kampong Gelam, which, in Raffles' time, was the area surrounding the Palace of the Sultan of Johor and its adjoining royal mosque. Kampong Gelam and the adjacent Rochor and Kallang area was an ancient and bustling port settlement. Here was where immigrant Malay communities from all over Nusantara would arrive and settle, alongside Chinese and Arab traders from further afield. And from here too, would local Malay communities set off by sailing vessel to the rest of Nusantara, or further beyond, to Mecca and the Haj.

The Palace of the Sultan, built by the British in 1843, still stands today and has been gazetted as a National Monument. It houses the Malay Heritage Centre, a museum that provides a deeper understanding into the history of the Malay peoples in Singapore. Just beside the former Palace compound sits Sultan Mosque, or Masjid Sultan, also gazetted a National Monument. A mosque has stood in this location since the 1820s, but this version was completed in 1928 and designed by Swan & Maclaren.

Masjid Sultan is a splendid example of the Indo-Saracenic style, combining traditional Mughal-Islamic elements, such as gleaming onion-shaped domes and twin minarets, with European architectural features. Inside the mosque is a large prayer hall, able to hold 5,000 devotees, and an intricate mausoleum where members of the Johor royal family are buried.

A visit during prayer time is an emotional experience, with thousands of devotees on their knees offering benedictions to God. Here, one observes clearly the role of Islam in the Malay world — how it is an integral part of Malay identity, and has, in the course of centuries, reached across to the many different Malay peoples, to bind them as one.

RIGHT: Sultan Mosque,
c. 1930s.

RIGHT: Chinese woman, early 20th century.

THE CHINESE

"The Chinese, who number eighty-six thousands out of a population of one hundred and thirty-nine thousand, are not only numerous enough, but rich and important enough to give Singapore the air of a Chinese town with a foreign settlement."

— Isabella Bird, *The Golden Chersonese and the Way Thither* (1883)

Next to arrive were the Chinese, who had been known in the islands of the Malay Archipelago for more than 1,000 years, ever since the southern kilns of the Tang Dynasty (7th to 9th century) began shipping their precious porcelain to the Middle East and beyond. In the galleries of the Asian Civilisations Museum sits proof of this trade — an entire ship of 9th-century pottery sunken *en route* to the Arab World in the waters just off Sumatra.

The Chinese came in waves to the Malay Peninsula and Singapore, with the first wave arriving with the treasure fleets of Cheng Ho in the 15th century. Many of them remained and intermarried with local Malay women, resulting in a unique hybrid community known as the Baba-Nyonya.

The second wave of Chinese were the Min-speaking coastal peoples of Fujian province in southern China. Known also as the Hokkiens, they were expert navigators and boat-builders — peoples of the sea. Cut off from the larger Chinese mainland by a series of mountain ranges, they took to the South China Sea from the 16th century onwards to survive. They became the principal traders in all the major port cities of Asia from the Coromandel Coast in India to Malacca, Bangkok, Batavia, Saigon, Phnom Penh, Manila, Canton, Macao and Nagasaki. Arriving in their junks from the grand port city of Quanzhou, they traded their fabulous silks, silver and lacquer from China for spices, sandalwood, ivory and other raw materials. And wherever they came, they settled in colonies of houseboats in sheltered bays, or, if they became wealthy, Chinese-style courtyard houses on the mainland. When the Portuguese — the first European colonisers in the East — arrived, they found the Hokkien already established.

The third wave of Chinese came as a result of European colonisation and the opening up of the so-called "treaty ports" along China's coast. Some backstory is in order here.

Between 1757 and 1842, all foreign traders to the Middle Kingdom were compelled, by Imperial Decree, to trade only at the Chinese port city of Canton (today's Guangzhou). For centuries, Canton had been one of the largest port cities in Asia, playing host to a cosmopolitan population of merchants and traders from the Middle East, India and the Malay Archipelago. The European traders came late in the game, and occupied a narrow sliver of land on the Canton waterfront, from which they would act as middlemen in the trade of luxury goods — silks, porcelain, lacquer and enamels — from China to Europe.

RIGHT: Portraits of Chinese communities, from *Zur Geschichte der Kostume (The History of Costumes)*, published in Munich, Germany by Braun & Schneider, 1880.

ABOUT: Chinese opium smokers, c. 1930.

The British, however, engaged in the trade of another, more sinister commodity — opium. In 1842, after almost a century of trade in opium, China had had enough of the drug that had hooked thousands of its subjects. It retaliated by burning a large shipment of the drug in the suburbs of Canton. The inevitable war that ensued was known as the First Opium War, and in the aftermath of the War, which China lost, a treaty was signed that forced the Middle Kingdom to open five port cities to international trade and to cede Hong Kong to Britain in perpetuity.

The five "treaty ports" were Canton, Amoy (Xiamen), Foochow (Fuzhou), Ningpo and Shanghai. They would be followed by some two dozen other treaty ports in the course of the mid-to-late 1800s, as China was forced to sign a series of humiliating unequal treaties with the other major Western Powers and Japan.

From the southern Chinese treaty ports of Canton, Amoy and Foochow, and to a lesser extent Ningpo and Shanghai, came the bulk of Singapore's Chinese population. They came as coolies and labourers in support of the bustling global trade that had taken root in Singapore and the rest of the Nanyang (南洋 or Southern Seas) region, as the Chinese referred to South-east Asia. Most came with nothing but the shirts and blouses on their backs, hoping to earn a living and return to their homeland. Some made their fortune — and stayed on as *towkays* (頭家) in their palatial houses.

The Chinese spoke, and continue to speak, a multiplicity of dialects, mutually unintelligible; in particular, the Chinese of the southern coastal provinces spoke variations on the Southern Min, or Min-nan (閩南) dialect, an ancient form of Chinese that dates back to the Tang Dynasty.

ABOVE: Thian Hock Keng Temple, early 20th century.

Most Chinese in Singapore, having come from the south of China, hail from three main dialect groups: the Hokkiens of Fujian province, by far the most numerous, who arrived by way of Fujian port cities like Amoy and Quanzhou; the Cantonese of Guangdong province, who arrived by way of the ports of Canton and Hong Kong; and the Teochew, who came from their ancestral lands in between today's Guangdong and Fujian provinces, and arrived by way of the port city of Swatow.

There were other minority dialect groups in Singapore, such as the Hokchiews, Hokchias and Henghuas, all of whom hail from the towns, villages and island settlements in the vicinity of the port city of Foochow. There were the Hakkas, scattered in small communities all over southern China and the descendants of Northern Chinese who had fled the lands of the Yellow River in late antiquity. There were the Hainanese, from their sub-tropical island homeland to the south of mainland China. And finally, there were the Shanghainese, who came later in the course of history, when the fall of the Qing Dynasty and civil unrest forced many to leave their city.

In the early years of colonial Singapore, most of the Chinese settled in the Telok Ayer area, around Telok Ayer Street, where can be found the greatest concentration of Nanyang-style shophouses; and where the oldest Chinese places of worship continue to be found today. These include the Fuk Tak Chi Temple, built by the Hakka and Cantonese communities in

RIGHT: Views of South Bridge Road (top) and North Bridge Road (bottom), c. 1930.

1824; the Thian Hock Keng Temple, erected by the Hokkien community in 1842 and dedicated to Mazu, or the Goddess of the Sea (gazetted as a National Monument in 1973); the Wak Hai Cheng Bio, built by the Teochew community in the 1850s (though the present building dates from 1896); and the tiny Siang Cho Keong Temple, built in 1868.

The street on which the last sits is known as Amoy Street, and it is a throwback to the days when the area was populated by thousands of immigrants from the port city of Amoy. Today, Telok Ayer street and the surrounding Tanjong Pagar, Kreta Ayer and Bukit Pasoh precincts are collectively known as Chinatown, in reference to the area being the heart of Chinese commercial and cultural activity for much of Singapore's history. In the meantime, Chinese continue to constitute the largest ethnic community in contemporary Singapore, accounting for just under 80 percent of the population.

THE INDIANS

"You strive hard in the island of Yava, which will be splendorous with seven kingdoms, like that even in Golden and Silver islands that are enwreathed with gold-mines, in and around Yava islands. On crossing over Yava Island, there is a mountain named Shishira, which touches heaven with its peak, and which gods and demons adore. You shall collectively rake through all the impassable mountains, waterfalls, and forests in these islands for the glorious wife of Rama."

— *The Ramayana*, Book 4

Indian influence in Southeast Asia dates back to classical antiquity, with ancient and continual trade relations existing between the various kingdoms of India and the polities of Southeast Asia. As early as the 2nd and 3rd century AD, Tamil epics and Buddhist works already referred to Indian traders travelling to Suvarnabhumi, or the Land of Gold, which, like Ptolemy's *Chersonesus Aurea* ("the Golden Chersonese") — coined, incidentally, in the same era — referred to the Malay Peninsula and its legendary riches.

As a result of trade, the kingdoms and empires of both continental and maritime Southeast Asia were Hindu-Buddhist in nature from as early as 200 BC to 1500 AD, with much of continental Southeast Asia today — Thailand, Myanmar, Laos and Cambodia — continuing to be Hindu-Buddhist states of an Indian variety (as opposed to Sinified Vietnam).

In fact, up until post World War II, the entire Southeast Asian region was referred to as either Further or Greater India, or the East Indies. The great Hindu epic, the *Ramayana*, is still venerated and performed today across

RIGHT: Portraits of Indian communities, from *Zur Geschichte der Kostume (The History of Costumes)*, published in Munich, Germany by Braun & Schneider, 1880.

continental Southeast Asia and in Java and Bali under the guise of various names such as the *Ramakien* or the *Yama Zatdaw*.

Very little specific archaeological and documentary evidence exists of early trade and exchange between India and Southeast Asia, though certainly by the 15th century, the port city of Malacca counted amongst its many traders and merchants, those from Gujarat, the Coromandel and Malabar Coasts and Bengal. In fact, it is believed that Gujarati merchants, who were Sufi Muslim, had been partly responsible for bringing Islam to Malacca and the Malay Archipelago. Around the same time, early communities of Tamil traders began settling in Malacca, intermarrying with local Malays and Chinese, thereby evolving a hybrid Chitty Melaka identity — the Indian equivalent of the Baba-Nyonya.

The Indian communities in Singapore arrived in a wave of migrations from the early 1800s, in particular because both India and Malaya (including Singapore) were under British colonial rule. Many Indians came initially as civil servants, as lascars and sepoys stationed in the Peninsula, or as convicts serving out their time. A proportion of Indians arriving in these shores were merchants, traders and moneylenders.

Like the Malay and Chinese communities, the Indian community was ethnically diverse. Most of the Indians who emigrated to Singapore were from the South and Sri Lanka (then known as Ceylon). The largest proportion was of Tamil descent. Even then, this sub-community was split into Tamil Hindus from Madras (Chennai), Pondicherry (Puducherry) and the Coromandel Coast (today's Tamil Nadu), whom the British administrators called *klings*; Tamil Muslims from the same region, whom the British called *chulias*; and Ceylonese or Jaffna Tamils from today's Sri Lanka.

The second largest community were the Malayalees from Kerala, who arrived by way of historic port cities such as Cochin (Kochi) and Calicut, which had been Portuguese, and then Dutch up until the British took over in 1795. The Punjabis, towering, statuesque people from the region of Punjab in the Northwest were another significant community. Many of them were Sikh, the men typically bearded, tall and strong, and sporting distinctive turbans.

The rest of the Indian community comprised a melting pot of ethnicities from central and north India, including Gujaratis, Sindhis, Sinhalese from Ceylon, Bengalis, Goans, Parsis, Telanganis, and Hindustanis from the North. All in all, the Singaporean Indian community spoke some dozen different languages, and also practised a range of different religions from Hinduism to Islam, Sikhism, Christianity, Jainism, Buddhism and Zoroastrianism.

Ethnicity also had something to do with employment in the Indian community. Ceylonese Tamils and Malayalees tended to be highly literate and English-educated, and thus came to take on jobs as civil servants

RIGHT: Sri Mariamman Temple, c. 1930s. Note the sepoys, now replaced, on the façade.

and writers. Gujaratis, Sindhis, Parsis and Tamil Muslims, with their long heritage of trade and historic trading networks, tended to be merchants. Sikhs were employed as policemen and doormen (the doorman of Raffles Hotel being an iconic example). Chettiars — Tamil Hindus from the Chettinaad area of the Coromandel Coast — came to be moneylenders.

The Indian community was originally settled to the north of South Bridge Road, at "Kampong Chulia", designated as such in Raffles' Town Plan. Two of the Indian community's most important places of worship continue to sit here along South Bridge Road.

The first is Sri Mariamman Temple, Singapore's oldest Hindu temple, founded in 1823, and built in 1843 by skilled craftsmen from India and China. It is dedicated to the worship of Sri Mariamman, a Hindu rain goddess unique to the Tamils and regarded as the goddess of the harvest, of fertility and of medicine. The temple is built in the traditional Dravidian style of Tamil Nadu, with its imposing *gopuram* or entrance tower depicting Hindu deities and beasts. The same basic form can be found in Hindu temples in the city of Chennai today; and temples such as this may be found in other port cities in Southeast Asia where the Tamils settled, including Penang, Yangon, Bangkok and Saigon.

Just down the street from Sri Mariamman Temple sits the Jamae Chulia Mosque, which catered to the religious needs of Tamil Muslims from the Coromandel Coast. Built in 1835, the mosque is an early example of the Eclectic style, with a primarily Indo-Saracenic form combining elements of Neoclassicism as well as adaptation for the tropical climate. Like Sri

FROM LEFT TO RIGHT:
Sikh sepoy, Parsi
merchant, Indian Muslim
gentleman. Late 19th to
early 20th century.

Mariamman Temple, the mosque's most imposing feature is its entrance, featuring a pair of seven-tiered octagonal minarets capped with onion-shaped domes. Above the doorway is a miniature Mughal Palace complete with doors and windows. Inside the mosque compound, one finds Tuscan columns and pilasters, alongside Chinese green-glazed tiles, all of which is set within a configuration of large verandas and windows that are architectural adaptations suited to the tropical weather.

Both temple and mosque were gazetted as National Monuments in 1973 and 1974 respectively, and continue to be lively, living places of worship for the local Indian community. A general visit on weekends and during the festival season finds them bustling with devotees and pilgrims.

From the mid 1800s, as the Kampong Chulia area quickly became overcrowded, later Indian immigrants began moving eastwards into the Serangoon area, what would later be known as "Little India".

From a semi-rural accumulation of dairy and cattle farms, Little India evolved to become the cultural and commercial heart of the local Indian community by the late 1800s, playing host to temples, bazaars and major Hindu festivals. It continues to play this role today, with the largest concentration of Indian businesses in Singapore — and throngs of Indian residents and visitors alike — concentrated inside a roughly rectangular area bounded by Race Course Road, Bukit Timah and Sungei Roads, Jalan Besar and Lavender Street.

The heart of Little India is Serangoon Road itself, which takes one all the way from the historic shophouse district around Campbell Street and Dunlop Street to the 24-hour hyper-supermarket that is Mustafa's — a national institution in its own right. The Indian Heritage Centre, located at the junction of Campbell Street and Clive Street presents a comprehensive history of the community, and the richness of its cultural heritage.

THE ARABS

"Oh Bringer of intimacy and happiness at the break of dawn
You drove from my heart a flame of impurity
I implore you to tell me, have you traversed the valley of al-Aqiq
And have you traversed the land of water and trees
A land of bountiful clouds, rainy
Where the earth is green with plants and flowers
I which rejoicing and happiness are perpetual
Oh what success for its settlers by goodness and victory."

— Habib Ali bin Muhammad al-Habshi, *Warid al-Uns* (probably late 1800s). Devotional ode by the poet and spiritual leader of the Alawi Sayyids of Hadhramaut. This is one of many odes sung during *zafin*, or devotional music and dance performances.

The Arab community in Singapore has always been small but influential. The community consists primarily of Hadhrami Arabs from the Hadhramaut region of what is Yemen today. This region is a narrow coastal strip along the southeastern edge of the Arabian Peninsula, with a climate that is dry and arid.

The harsh landward conditions turned the Hadhramis towards the sea, and, for centuries, they have had a tradition of seafaring and maritime trade, primarily in the Indian Ocean, where they have taken their wares — dates, perfumes and precious frankincense — to the fabled African and Indian port cities of Zanzibar, Dar Es Salaam, Mombasa, Cambay (in Gujarat) and the Malabar Coast.

RIGHT: Portraits of Arab gentlemen, late 19th century to early 20th century.

ABOVE: Junction of Arab Street and North Bridge Road, mid 20th century.

Spiritually, the Hadhramis practised a form of Sufi, or mystical Islam, which propounded a more personal, rather than institutional, relationship with God. They belonged to the Ba 'Alawi ("order of Alawi") *tariqah*, which was also a form of genealogy, in that the practitioners of the order were all distantly related to the founding patriarch.

Wherever they went, the Hadhramis brought with them their traditions of Alawiyya Sufism, and it is possible that they too had a hand to play in the Islamisation of parts of the Indian coast and the Malay Archipelago. The most wealthy and influential of the Hadhrami families were *sayyids* — descendants of the Prophet Muhammad himself — and were regarded as having noble lineage. They received privileged treatment wherever they went in the East, with many of them marrying into local royalty or becoming community leaders.

The Hadhramis in Singapore arrived mostly from the early 19th century, when the Hadhramaut region was ruled as a British Protectorate. From the port city of Aden, an important port in global trading routes, some thousands of the Hadhramis left for cities in the East Indies, in particular the Straits Settlements towns of Penang, Malacca and Singapore, but also the major cities in Java and Sumatra — Batavia, Soerabaja and Palembang.

In Singapore, the Arabs settled in their own "campong" designated by Raffles in his Town Plan, in the vicinity of the Royal Compound under the suzerainty of the Sultan of Johor. Here, they set up shops selling perfumes and unguents, dates and frankincense. Today, this area is known as Arab Street, and has evolved into a rather distinctive and dynamic mix of local Malay and pan-Middle Eastern (Egyptian, Lebanese, Yemeni, Turkish) food establishments.

RIGHT: Alsagoff Arab
School.

The Arab community of primarily merchants and entrepreneurs was a formidable economic force in the colony. They specialised in retail, wholesale, real estate and travel for the Haj, or pilgrimage to Mecca. In particular, a few *sayyid* Alawi families established themselves as major land owners and philanthropists, and would figure strongly in Singapore's history.

The Alsagoff (*al-Saqqaaf*) family of the merchant house Alsagoff & Co owned swathes of land in Beach Road, including the original plot on which Raffles Hotel was built. At one time they owned a large sprawling bungalow and grounds in Kampong Rochor, sitting adjacent to the still-standing Hajjah Fatimah Mosque. That estate was demolished in the early 1970s in a wave of urban rejuvenation. All that remains of the Alsagoff family's presence in the area is the Alsagoff Arab School, established in 1912 to teach Islamic knowledge, the Arabic language and English to the Malay-Muslim community.

The Aljunieds (*al-Junayd*), a Hadhrami family from Palembang, owned large tracts of land in the High Street and Victoria Street area, and in what is today the Aljunied district in north-eastern Singapore. The patriarch of the family, Syed Omar bin Ali Aljunied, is the founder of the Masjid Omar Kampong Melaka, the oldest mosque in Singapore established in 1820. He also donated land towards the construction of St Andrew's Church.

Finally, the Alkaffs (*al-Kaaf*) of Alkaff & Co, were spice traders. They built the Alkaff Arcade, Singapore's first indoor shopping arcade, on the Singapore waterfront. Designed by Swan & Maclaren in an iconic Moorish style and erected in 1909, it was the first building to rise more than two storeys on the waterfront. It was demolished in 1978. The Alkaff family's legacy remains in the form of Alkaff Mansion, built in 1918 by the family as a weekend mansion on top of Telok Blangah hill. A Tudor-style colonial bungalow, it was known for hosting high society parties in the 1930s.

Prominent Arabs in Singapore history are not limited to businessmen alone. One of the most mercurial characters in the community was Sayyid Noh bin Sayyid Mohamad bin Sayyid Ahmad Al-Habshi, or Habib Noh, for short. A Sufi saint and a *sayyid*, he arrived in Singapore in 1819 and became a very well-known and respected figure in the Muslim community. He was notorious for being a Robin Hood of sorts, stealing from proprietors and shopkeepers to give to the poor. Popular belief had it that he was endowed with magical abilities, such as being able to perform miracle healing on children, and to translocate himself to far-flung locations like Mecca.

He passed away in 1866, and a shrine was built over his tomb which was placed on the top of Mount Palmer. Today, the Keramat Habib Noh still stands on the peak of Mount Palmer, and, for more than a century, has attracted pilgrims en route to the Haj from the Netherlands East Indies and even as far away as China.

Today, the Arab community in Singapore continues to be small. Save the most prominent members of the community, many Singapore Arabs and their families have assimilated themselves well, often due to intermarriage into Malay culture so as to be indistinguishable to the ordinary eye from their Malay-Muslim brethren. The loss of Singaporean Arab identity continues to be an issue of concern to the community.

RIGHT: Masjid Omar Kampong Melaka, c. 1920.

FAR RIGHT: Keramat Habib Noh, mid 20th century.

THE EURASIANS

"Nor eastward far though fair Malacca lie,
Her groves embosom'd in the morning sky;
Though with her am'rous sons the valiant line
Of Java's isle in battle rank combine,
Though poison'd shafts their pond'rous quivers store;
Malacca's spicy groves and golden ore,
Great Albuquerque, thy dauntless toils shall crown!"

— Luís Vaz de Camões, *Os Lusíadas* (1572)

The Eurasians are the descendants of the various European traders, merchants and colonial powers who, arriving in Asia, settled down, inter-married with local Asian communities, and evolved unique, hybrid cultures and traditions that fused East and West.

In Singapore, there are three distinct Eurasian communities. The first, largest, and the oldest are the Kristang, or the Portuguese Eurasians, descendants of those Portuguese conquistadors and traders who arrived more than 500 years ago in Malacca. Speaking a *patois* entirely their own, also named kristang, and fusing Portuguese and Malay words, they remain a significant presence in Singapore society today. In particular, the Portuguese Eurasians are known for their fiery cuisine — *curry debal*, also known as Devil's Curry, being a prime example — that fused Portuguese methods of cooking with Malay spices.

The Kristang are Roman Catholic, and in the old days, were equally at home with western dress as in sarong kebaya; equally comfortable with

RIGHT: Wedding of
Stephen A Pereira and
Nita E Fernandez,
1 March 1938.

ABOVE: Portrait of Eurasian girl, 1930s.

BELOW: Singapore Recreation Club, c. 1910s.

English which they always spoke (or attempted to speak) as well as an Englishman, plus Malay and Kristang. Some last names of the community include D'Almeida, Da Silva, De Cruz, Oliveiro and Rozario.

Five hundred years on, their traditions still hold strong as they continue to celebrate religious festivals and Portuguese-origin songs and dances. They share a common heritage with Portuguese Eurasians elsewhere, most notably the Indo-Portuguese in Goa, the Kristang in Malacca and the Macanese in Macao, all of which have hybrid languages and cuisine.

The second oldest Eurasian community is that of the Dutch Eurasians, known as Indos in their ancestral homeland of the Netherlands East Indies (today's Indonesia). Historic photographs from the suburbs of Batavia and Soerabaja depict these mixed-race families, the women or *nyonya besar* dressed in elaborate sarong and kebaya and the men in white suits and shirts, as they pose for family portraits on the verandas of their Indies-style bungalows.

In Singapore, the Dutch Eurasian community is very small; it originates from Malacca and Sri Lanka (former Ceylon) which was, for a time, also a Dutch colony. It continues to play host to a significant community of Dutch Burghers today. Some last names of the community include Cornelius, Danker, Klass and Westerhout.

Finally, there are the Anglo-Eurasians (Anglo-Chinese, Anglo-Malays and Anglo-Indians), who emerged in Singapore somewhat later in the course of British rule. These are the descendants of the British (including the Scottish and Irish) officers and traders in the colony; though there are certainly also Eurasian descendants of other Europeans — Germans, French,

Danish — who arrived in Singapore during the British era. Some last names of this community include Clarke, Moss, Barker and Sheares.

The most significant physical legacy of the Eurasians today is the Singapore Recreation Club, established in 1883 on the north end of the Padang. After the Singapore Cricket Club, which was notably Europeans-only, the Singapore Recreation Club was perhaps the most exclusive club in Singapore. It was primarily a sports club, with a focus on cricket and hockey. Post-independence, in 1963, the Club opened its doors to non-Eurasians, though Eurasians continue to make up a significant proportion of its membership. In 1997, the former clubhouse was replaced with a brand-new one.

The Eurasian enclave in Singapore was historically centred around Waterloo and Queen Streets and Selegie Road, where the Jewish community had also been located. The place of worship most related to the community is St Joseph's Church, which was the home of the Portuguese Mission, and had links with Macao. The present church building was built in 1912 in a Neo-Gothic style with distinctive Portuguese blue and white *azulejo* tiles adorning the front façade. It was gazetted as a National Monument in 2005.

Elsewhere in Singapore, the heart of Eurasian culture is held to be at Katong, on the East Coast of Singapore, once an idyllic seaside suburb of opulent weekend villas and mansions. Here and in nearby Joo Chiat may be found the few remaining restaurants that serve Eurasian cuisine. The Eurasian Association, founded in 1919, has a clubhouse here, and its small but comprehensive Eurasian Heritage Centre provides an overview of the history of this community.

More recently, with the rise of marriages between Singaporeans and expatriate Europeans and Americans, a fourth new and completely distinct community of Eurasian-Singaporeans — Singaporeans of mixed race — has emerged. It has very little to do with the traditional Eurasian communities in Singapore, but sports a rather more contemporary, global, pop culture-influenced outlook of life. The emergence of these New Eurasians has thrown into question the meaning of being "Eurasian"; at the same time it adds to the diversity of Singapore society and ensures it continues to retain a unique, hybrid flavour.

St. Joseph's Church, c. 1930.

"Kwan Kong dengan ber-triak skwat kwat, ada ber-maki sama Soong Khuan; dia kata, 'lumata-biru punya budak-kichil! Janggot-ungu (atan umu) punya bangsa-tikus! Goa sama Low Höng Siok ada mang-aku man-jadi adek-bradek di [käbon] Tho Wan, dengan manarok sumpa mau kah tundok sama lu yang ada mongkirati pada negri HAN punya punchuri-duraka, handak man-jadi sa-wäng goa ya? Goa säkarang suda ter-käna di akal-panipu, chuma ada ma-nanti mati saja — suda! Buat apa lu banyak mulot lagi?'"

— *Chrita Dahulu-kala, Namanya Sam Kok, Atau, Tiga Negri Ber-prang: Siok, Gwi, Sama Gor di Jaman "Han Teow"* Volume XX. (1892–1896). Baba-Malay translation of the Chinese epic, *The Romance of the Three Kingdoms*. Translated by Batu Gantong.

RIGHT: Peranakan Wedding, around 1920. Photograph, gelatin silver print. Produced by the Lee Brothers.

Where "Eurasian" refers to communities of mixed European and Asian parentage, "Peranakan" refers to communities of mixed Asian parentage. The term itself literally means "of the soil" and refers to native-born (ie born in the Malay Archipelago) foreign immigrant communities. It was used eventually to refer to mixed-race Asian communities, and, more recently, even more specifically used in reference to the Chinese-Peranakans, or Baba-Nyonya, also known as the Straits Chinese or Peranakan Cina.

The Baba-Nyonya are certainly the most well-known and populous of the Peranakan communities, with many families counting amongst the most wealthy, elite and influential in Singapore, and the cities of the former Straits Settlements, Penang and Malacca.

Some believe that the Baba-Nyonya are descended from Chinese traders and sailors who came on board the vast treasure fleets commanded by Ming Admiral Cheng Ho in the 14th century. Stopping over in the port city of Malacca, many of the Chinese remained behind, and intermarried with local Malay women, creating, in the course of centuries, a rich, hybrid culture and tradition that fused southern Chinese (Hokkien and Teochew) religion, ritual and superstition with local Malay elements.

They spoke Baba Malay – a variant of Malay with Hokkien and Teochew phrases thrown in, and chewed *sireh*, the mild stimulant that is used all over the Malay Archipelago and India as a form of social ritual. They evolved their own unique cuisine, blending Chinese staples and meats, in particular pork, with local Malay spices and ingredients, such as *buah keluak*, galangal (blue ginger), tamarind and coconut.

The material culture of the Baba-Nyonya is rich and heady, and entirely distinct from anything else in Asia. Wealthy families were extremely fond of elaborate styles of architecture, furniture and fashion that blended not only Chinese and Malay aesthetic styles, but also European elements like pediments and pilasters. In particular, the women of the family — matriarchs, all of them — were known for their splendid lace and batik sarong kebaya and beaded slippers and for their *kerongsang*, large gold and silver pendants that hung on their bosoms and were a demonstration of wealth.

Peranakans are also known for their colourful and elaborate porcelain, or Nyonya-ware, commissioned in sets of 144 individual pieces for the elaborate *tok panjang* or family banquet. Entire sets would be commissioned in bright pink, green or turquoise porcelain with exuberantly depicted auspicious symbols like peonies, phoenixes and butterflies. In particular, the *kamcheng*, or bowl with a lid, holds its own as perhaps the most iconic form of *pingan mangkok* (kitchen-ware). The Peranakan Museum in Singapore has perfectly preserved and captured the art and material culture of this unique community.

The most wealthy Baba-Nyonya families settled in the Emerald Hill area; and the many residential shophouse-villas, or *rumah kiah-kay* on

FROM LEFT TO RIGHT:
Dresser, Penang, teak,
early 20th century;
kerongsang, Trengganu,
early 20th century; *kasut
manek* (beaded slippers),
Myanmar, early – mid
20th century; kamcheng,
China late 19th to early
20th century.

Emerald Hill, immaculately conserved and restored, bear witness to past glories. Meanwhile, the heart of living Peranakan culture is at Joo Chiat, a conservation district on the East Coast of Singapore. It was here that many wealthy Peranakans established seaside villas and mansions in the early to mid 1900s, and here also, particularly on Joo Chiat Road, one finds dozens of spectacular Peranakan-style residential shophouses. Needless to say, Joo Chiat is also known for the most authentic Peranakan food.

Aside from the Baba-Nyonya, the other two Peranakan communities of note are the Jawi Peranakans and the Chitty Melaka, both of which are of mixed Tamil and Malay parentage, but with the former being Muslim and the latter being Hindu. Like the Baba-Nonya, they settled primarily in the Straits Settlement towns of Singapore, Penang and Malacca and evolved a unique food and material culture that blended elements of Tamil, Chinese and Malay tradition. The Chitty Melaka, in particular, are distinct from Tamil communities in that they are the descendants of Tamil merchants that had lived and traded in Malacca during the time of the Sultanate.

Unfortunately, due to inter-marriage with the Malay and Indian communities, both Indian Peranakan communities are at risk of disappearing altogether. Chitty Road, in Little India, makes reference to a former community of the Chitty Melaka that used to reside in the area. In the meantime, the story of the Jawi Peranakans is told, albeit briefly, at the Peranakan Museum.

THE BRITISH (AND OTHER EUROPEANS)

"KNOW YE THEREFORE, that we, greatly tendering the Honour of our Nation, the Wealth of our People, and the Encouragement of them, and others of our loving Subjects in their good Enterprizes, for the Increase of our Navigation, and the Advancement of lawful Traffick, to the Benefit of our Common Wealth, have of our especial Grace, certain Knowledge, and mere Motion, given and granted, and by these Presents, for us, our Heirs and Successors, do give and grant unto our said loving Subjects, before in these Presents expressly named, that they and every of them from henceforth be, and shall be one Body Corporate and Politick, in Deed and in Name, by the Name of The Governor and Company of Merchants of London, Trading into the East-Indies..."

— Charter granted by Queen Elizabeth I to the East India Company. Dated the 31st of December, in the 43rd year of Her Reign. Anno Domini, 1600.

Europeans made their appearance in these Eastern waters in the early 1500s, lured by trade in those odoriferous spices — nutmeg, mace, cloves and pepper — that could be found nowhere else but in the thousand islands of the Malay Archipelago.

The Portuguese and Spanish were the first to arrive, in the 1500s. The Portuguese came east by way of Africa and India; the Spanish, west by way of the Americas. They founded their settlements, namely Malacca and Manila, and set down roots that endured for the next 500 years.

The Dutch were the next to arrive. Merchants of the Vereenigde Oost-Indische Compagnie (VOC), or the United Dutch East India Company, came

RIGHT: British gentlemen with Chinese servants, late 19th century.

ABOVE: Portrait of John Crawfurd, c. 1850s.

in their East Indiamen (the Dutch equivalent to the Spanish and Portuguese galleons) and, in 1619, took the city of Batavia. They remained for 350 years.

Some 150 years later, the British finally arrived in their frigates. Like the Dutch, they were merchants, belonging to a joint-stock company based in London, the Honourable East India Company, which had already, in the mid-to-late 1600s, established a toehold along the coasts of India, most notably the ports of Bombay, Madras and Calcutta.

In 1786, the Company acquired Penang from the Sultan of Kedah. Determined to counter growing Dutch influence in the East Indies, the Company — through the machinations of the Messrs Raffles and Farquhar — subsequently acquired Singapore in 1819. Both colonies, and Malacca, were administered together as the Straits Settlements, with the capital in Singapore from 1832.

In 1858, the East India Company was dissolved and its properties taken over by the British Crown. The Straits Settlements, including Singapore, became a Crown Colony, directly administered from the Colonial Office in London. This continued until 1942 and the outbreak of World War II.

The typical impression of colonial life in British Malaya and Singapore is that of the leisurely, gentry-like merchant or civil servant family in their black-and-white bungalow. It was the world of the *sahib* and the *memsahib*, with their children, servants and ayahs, having tea parties on the lawn and elaborate dinners in their expansive verandas. But the fact was that in the early years of the settlement, life was harsh and travel to the far-off East Indies was long and difficult. As a result, the British population in Singapore was predominantly male — merchants, military and mercenaries — who had left the cities of London, Manchester and Liverpool to seek their fortune abroad.

Surprisingly, the initial wave of British pioneers and settlers in Singapore saw a significant proportion of Scots. The first two Residents of Singapore,

RIGHT: British gentlemen, 1896.

FAR RIGHT: British ladies — Mrs Swettenham and Mrs Anson, late 19th century.

TOP: View of Bras Basah Road, with St Joseph's Institution at right, early 20th century.

BELOW: Singapore Swimming Club, early 20th century.

Major Farquhar (1774–1839; residency 1819–1823) and his successor, Dr John Crawfurd (1783–1868; residency 1823–1826), were Scots, as were the founders of many of the earliest (and still remaining) trading houses, for example, Guthrie & Co and Fraser & Co. It is notable that St Andrew's Church, the colony's most prominent European place of worship in the early years, was named after the patron saint of Scotland, its construction having been funded by Scottish traders.

Small numbers of women did begin to arrive in the settlement, however, and depictions of life at the turn of the 19th century presented men and women in full-on Victorian garb: the men with their beards and moustaches and double-breasted suits, and women in severe gowns with corseted waists and bustled skirts. These soon proved completely inappropriate for the tropical weather, and were replaced, after World War I, by far more practical apparel — light cottons, muslins and linen, always in white or variations of white in order to reduce the effect of the stifling heat.

Nostalgia was rife in colonial society. Cut off from their homeland, the British in Singapore attempted to replace the untamable jungle with recreated elements of the familiar. The heart of the city was erected in the image of the imperial city itself — London, or rather, Liverpool, with its bustling international port and Neo-Classical edifices; and where many of the British would have set sail in the ships of the Peninsula & Oriental (P & O), Cunard and other liners.

Just beyond the city were the expansive plantations and sprawling estates of the new gentry, created in the image of those country estates in England and Scotland, with their bungalows scattered amidst large, verdant gardens and estates suggesting the British countryside. The names of the streets taking one through the suburbs — country lanes almost with names like Orchard Road, Tanglin Road and Balmoral Road — certainly reinforced the illusion that the colony was a kind of Britain transplanted to the East.

Social life in the city also resembled that in Britain with the Club being at the centre of society. Initially there were gentlemen's clubs and sports clubs, like the Singapore Cricket Club and the Singapore Turf Club. Swimming Clubs and Sailing Clubs, suited to the tropical weather, soon followed suit. And then there were the grand hotels which were the centre of the fashionable set and where one would go for elegant soirées and balls.

For many of the colony's newly arrived, the allure of such a lifestyle was dizzying, particularly as many were from a middle class or lower-middle class background in Britain. The whirl of colonial society from club to hotel, and the lap of luxury to be had in the colonial villa with its bevy of servants, was a dream for most, and one of the surest routes to upward mobility.

The British weren't the only Europeans in Singapore, of course. The French had also established a modest but significant presence in the colony, establishing its most important Roman Catholic places of worship and education. This includes the Cathedral of the Good Shepherd (Singapore's first Catholic Church, 1847), St Joseph's Institution (Singapore's first Catholic school, 1852) and the Convent of the Holy Infant Jesus (1854) in the Bras Basah area, all of which are National Monuments today.

The Germans and Austrians also had a modest presence in the settlement, with their most visible legacy being the former Teutonia Club, built in 1900 and designed by R A J Bidwell of Swan & Maclaren. Today it is the Goodwood Park Hotel, the structure is also a National Monument.

Finally, there were also the Irish, who counted, amongst them, some of Singapore's early architects, most notably George Drumgold Coleman, who was responsible for much of early Singapore's urban landscape, and Denis Santry of Swan & Maclaren, whose most notable building is the Indo-Saracenic Sultan Mosque in Kampong Gelam.

The Jews

"A small party of Jews from Persia and Turkey ... have lately settled in this place, with whom we have had occasional conversations.... They ha(ve) travelled over many parts of Europe and Asia, and some of them display more than ordinary candour and intelligence."

— Jacob Tomlin, *A Missionary Journal kept at Singapore and Siam from May 1830, to January 1832* (1832)

The Jews of Singapore, though a very small community, have figured largely in its development as a thriving port city and commercial hub of Asia. They are Baghdadi Jews, with a heritage dating back to the 8th century, when Baghdad, the capital of the Abbasid Empire in Iraq, was a bustling cosmopolitan trade centre and crossroads of civilisations.

In the early 1800s, the Ottoman governor of Baghdad, Daud Pasha began to persecute Jews, and many of the most prominent of the community took to the nearby (British) East India Company trading ports in India — Bombay, Madras, Calcutta. The Baghdadi trade diaspora eventually also made its presence felt in the Far East, particularly in Rangoon (Yangon), Shanghai and Singapore.

Singapore's Baghdadi Jewish community came by way of Calcutta very early on in the colony's settlement. By the 1830s, it was already established in sufficient numbers to be able to build a synagogue with a proper *minyan*, or quorum of ten men to hold prayer services. Though that original synagogue is long gone, the street where it was sited is still called Synagogue Street.

BELOW: *Birchot Shamayim, Customs of the Jews of Iraq*, Baghdad/Livorno, 1928.

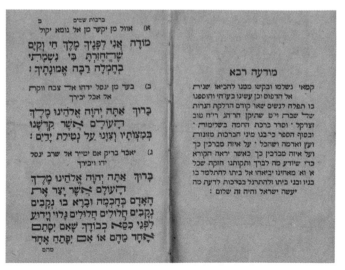

ABOVE: Baghdadi Jewish girl, early 20th century.

OPPOSITE TOP: Chesed-El Synagogue, early 20th century.

OPPOSITE BOTTOM: Maghain Aboth Synagogue, mid 20th century.

Outwardly, the Baghdadi Jews looked Arabian and spoke a version of Arabic. They were Orthodox Jews, eating kosher, adhering strictly to the teachings of the Torah and holding their liturgy in Hebrew. Through trading in gems, spices, porcelain, cotton and, in particular, opium, some of the trading families became exceedingly wealthy and influential.

A second wave of Jewish immigration to the colony took place between 1870 and 1900, with the opening of the Suez Canal. Many of the new arrivals were Ashkenazi or European Jews, as opposed to the Baghdadi Jews who were Sephardic; though Baghdadi Jews continued to arrive from Calcutta, Bombay and even from Iraq itself. The community swelled to a few hundred by the early 1900s. Many of the most wealthy began, at the time, to abandon their traditional Arab dress and ways of living, and to adopt British customs, dress and education.

In 1878, a new synagogue was built on Waterloo Street to cater to the spiritual needs of the burgeoning community. Called Maghain Aboth, or "Shield of Our Fathers", it is the oldest synagogue in Singapore and in Southeast Asia. Gazetted as a National Monument today, the original trustees were two of Singapore's most important Jewish patriarchs: Abraham Solomon and Manasseh Meyer.

Meyer, in particular, is remembered well in Singapore. He became the most wealthy Jewish merchant and real estate mogul in the Far East, owning large tracts of land and properties in Singapore, including hotels and palatial private villas on Oxley Rise and along the Katong waterfront. In 1905, Meyer built a private synagogue, Chesed-El (or "Merciful God") on the grounds of his Belle Vue estate on Oxley Rise. Designed by R A J Bidwell of Swan & Maclaren, it was open to the broader Jewish community and still stands today although Belle Vue itself has been demolished. It is also a National Monument.

Elsewhere, the Jewish legacy remains in the form of a pair of buildings bearing the Star of David on their façades in the Bras Basah area. These are the Ellison Building on Selegie Road, built by Ashkenazi Jewish trader Isaac Ellison in 1924, and the David Elias Building on Middle Road, built by merchant David Elias in 1928. The area itself, sitting at the confluence of Middle Road, Selegie Road, Short Street and Wilkie Road, was once the *mahallah*, or heart of middle- and working-class Jewish residential and commercial life.

Having swelled to almost 2,000-strong by 1945, the Jewish community took a blow during and in the aftermath of World War II, with many families emigrating to Australia, England, the United States and the new state of Israel. Their legacy is still felt in the many streets named after the pioneering patriarchs — Solomon Street, Meyer Road, Adis Road, Elias Road, Frankel Road and Penhas Road being some of them. In the meantime, a small number of old families continue to remain today in Singapore as some of the city-state's most influential business leaders.

THE ARMENIANS

"This small but elegant building does great credit to the public spirit and religious feeling of the Armenians of this settlement; for we believe that few instances could be shewn where so small a community have contributed funds sufficient for the erection of a similar edifice [...] the Armenian Church is one of the most ornate and best-finished pieces of architecture that this settlement can boast of."

— *The Singapore Free Press*, 17 March 1836

As a community, the Armenians of Singapore were even smaller than the Jews. They were Persian Armenians, in that they hailed from a small enclave of Armenians in New Julfa, Isfahan; settled there since the 1600s, in the reign of the Safavid Shahs of Iran. Since ancient times, the Armenians have formed trade diasporas, leaving their ancestral homeland of Armenia in the Caucasus mountains and traversing land and sea to markets as far off as Changan in Tang China.

The merchants of New Julfa were shrewd merchants and intermediaries, primarily in the Persian silk trade. They enjoyed great privilege at the courts of the Shahs and were known for their hardworking nature and their thrift. When the Safavid dynasty fell in 1736, however, a wave of persecution forced many to leave New Julfa for the British trading ports in India, chiefly Bombay, Madras and Calcutta. In this, their history is very similar to that of the Baghdadi Jews.

Also like the Jews, the Armenians in Singapore and Malaya arrived by way of Calcutta which was then the most important trading port in British

BELOW LEFT: Armenian bride and groom, 1920s.

BELOW RIGHT: The Armenian Apostolic Church of St Gregory the Illuminator, mid 20th century.

RIGHT TOP: Adelphi Hotel, early 20th century.

RIGHT BOTTOM: Raffles Hotel, late 19th century.

India; and they always came very soon after the British had settled. Briefly settling in Penang at the turn of the 18th century, they moved on to Singapore to put down roots.

The Singaporean community was minuscule, never numbering more than a few hundred at any one time. But there were enough of them to form a sizeable presence in downtown Singapore, in the vicinity of today's Bras Basah area. They retained strong links of kinship and business with the larger Armenian diaspora in the region, particularly in Calcutta, but also in Burma, Siam, the Philippines, the Netherlands East Indies and China.

In 1836, the Armenian Apostolic Church of St Gregory of the Illuminator opened its doors along Armenian Street to serve a small congregation. Designed by George Drumgold Coleman, it was one of the earliest churches established in the colony, and is certainly the oldest church still standing in Singapore today. It was gazetted a National Monument in 1973.

RIGHT: Joe Constantine, manager of Raffles Hotel, Arshak Sarkies, Martin Sarkies and Martyrose Arathoon (manager of the Adelphi Hotel later on).

The Armenians of Singapore counted amongst them numerous significant traders, businessmen and hoteliers, the most well-known of whom were the Sarkies Brothers. Persian Armenians from New Julfa, the four brothers made their way separately to the East Indies by way of Calcutta. Martin, the eldest, was the first to arrive in Malaya. He was followed by Tigran, who co-founded with his elder brother the Eastern & Oriental Hotel in Penang in 1885, also the year the brothers founded the company "Sarkies Brothers" proper.

In 1887, Martin and Tigran established their most famous still-standing legacy — Raffles Hotel in Singapore. Their third brother, Aviet, went on to establish the Strand Hotel in Rangoon in 1901. And, finally, Arshak, the youngest, arrived to take over the management reins of the E & O (as it is affectionately called) in Penang.

By the turn of the 19th century, the Sarkies Brothers were arguably the leading hoteliers in the East, counting, amongst their properties, not just Raffles, the E & O and the Strand, but also the Crag Hotel in Penang, as well as the Seaview Hotel in Singapore. A cousin managed the nearby Adelphi Hotel in Singapore with a consortium of Armenian partners, while a

Javanese branch of the Sarkies' family, headed by Martin's son, Lucas Martin Sarkies, went on to helm the fabled Oranje Hotel in the port city of Soerabaja. The descendants of the main Malayan branch of the family continue to live in Singapore and Penang today.

Another famous Armenian was Ms Agnes Joaquim, who was born in Singapore and died in the late 1800s. An avid horticulturalist, Ms Joaquim cultivated the first Vanda orchid hybrid.

RELIGIONS AND FESTIVALS

Ten major world religions have historically been represented in Singapore's multicultural and multi-religious social fabric. These are Hinduism, Judaism, Zoroastrianism, Buddhism, Taoism, Jainism, Christianity, Islam, Sikhism and the Baha'i Faith. Of these, four have their origins in India, five in the Middle and Near East, and the remaining one in China.

Almost all of these religions have deep roots in Singapore's cosmopolitan multicultural port society, having made their way through networks of trade and immigration. Except for the Baha'i Faith, all religions have places of worship that were established from the mid to late 1800s, and many of these places of worship have been gazetted as National Monuments. All of these religions are still practiced in Singapore today.

A diversity of religions means a diversity of festivals and feast days observed and celebrated by the various religious communities in Singapore, making for a varied, colourful and boisterous year-round festival calendar.

Seven religious festivals are celebrated as national public holidays. These include the Chinese Lunar New Year, which marks the end of winter and the

RIGHT: Chinese New Year festivities, late 19th century.

CLOCKWISE FROM TOP LEFT: *Koran*, probably Indonesia, 18th or 19th century; Crucifix, the Philippines, 17th century; Shi Hou Guanyin, China, Yuan – Early Ming Dynasty (14th /15th century); Somaskanda, Tamil Nadu, Chola Period (c. 1200).

beginning of Spring; Christmas and Good Friday, the latter marking Christ's crucifixion and death at Calvary; the Muslim festivals of Eid al-Fitr (known as Hari Raya Puasa in Malay), which marks the end of the fasting month of Ramadan and Eid al-Adha (known as Hari Raya Haji), which commemorates Abraham's sacrifice of Ishmael; the Hindu Deepavali or Festival of Lights (known as Diwali in India), which celebrates the triumph of good over evil; and Vesak Day, the anniversary of Buddha's birth.

Besides these public holidays, the various communities also observe other festivals. The Chinese celebrate the Mid-Autumn Festival around September, observing festivities by eating mooncakes and — specifically in Singapore and Malaysia — carrying brightly lit lanterns while admiring the full moon. The Dragon Boat Festival occurs around May and commemorates the death of the poet and minister Qu Yuan in the Warring States Period. During the festival, the Chinese eat specially made dumplings known as *zongzi*, and up until the 1980s, also staged elaborate dragonboat races along the Singapore waterfront.

The Hungry Ghost Festival is one festival that is celebrated with particular zeal by Chinese in Singapore and Malaya. The Chinese believe that during the Seventh Month of the Lunar calendar when this festival takes

RIGHT: Man with kavadi during Thaipusam, c. 1930s.

place, the Gates of Hell are cast open, and the ghosts of the deceased emerge to revisit their past homes and relatives. In order to appease these spirits, Chinese families make offerings and prepare elaborate feasts; and the streets of Chinese neighbourhoods typically come alive with *getai* performances — energetic performances of Chinese opera, popular song and street theatre.

Muslims in Singapore, who are largely Sunni Muslims, observe the month of Ramadan during which no healthy man or woman may consume food or any liquid, not even water, in the hours between sunrise and sunset. Maulud Nabi, or the birthday of the Prophet Muhammad, is also celebrated and used to involve large-scale street parades up until the 1960s.

Hindus celebrate Thaipusam, a feast of sacrifice and offering, where devotees have to go through a gruelling process of bearing *kavadis*, elaborate ritual structures literally pierced and skewered through the flesh and the tongues of the bearer. Thai Pongal, a harvest festival unique to communities from Tamil Nadu is celebrated in January: this sees Tamil households decorating the entrance of their houses with *kolam*, or coloured rice flour. Theemithi, or the Fire-walking Festival, is observed around October, and sees devotees observing a ritual of walking over pits of burning coal.

Christians, particularly Catholics, observe all the major Catholic feast days, including Lent and Easter in March, the Ascension (of the Lord) and the Pentecost in May, the Assumption of the Virgin Mary in August, All Saints' Day in November, and the Feast of the Immaculate Conception in December.

Aside from these festivals, the other religious communities also observe important days, such as Vesakhi, or the Sikh New Year; the Jain Paryushan, or fasting week; Nowruz, or the Iranian New Year; and Rosh Hashanah or the Jewish New Year.

STREETS OF HARMONY

Perhaps the most tangible expression of Singapore's multiculturalism is the existence, in downtown Singapore, of numerous "streets of harmony". These are single streets on which are to be found places of worship of major world religions, often sitting side by side.

The first, one of the oldest streets in Singapore, is Telok Ayer Street, which, in the 1800s to the early 1900s, used to front the harbour (its name means "bay water" in Malay). This was where Chinese and Indian immigrants first set foot on the island. As a result, it is home to some of the oldest temples, mosques and churches, as well as clan associations.

The list includes the Thian Hock Keng Temple (1842), one of the oldest Chinese temples in Singapore; the Al-Abrar Mosque (1855), which served the religious needs of the Chulia, or Indian Muslim community; the former Nagore Durgah Shrine (1830), dedicated to a Sufi saint; the Telok Ayer Chinese Methodist Church (1925), serving Chinese Christians; the Ying Fo Fui Kun (1844), the Hakka Clan Association; and the former Keng Teck Whay which was a Hokkien Peranakan Association (1856). Notably, all of these places of worship and historic clan associations are National Monuments today.

Here, also, sits another significant Clan Association, namely the Hokkien Huay Kuan or the Hokkien clan association, alongside dozens of early

RIGHT: View down Telok Ayer Street, early 20th century.

RIGHT: Cathedral of the Good Shepherd, early 20th century.

1900s Nanyang-style shophouses in a range of architectural styles: Eclectic, Chinese baroque and Art Deco. They were used by the mixed Chinese, Indian Muslim and Hindu communities resident on the street.

The second street — actually a pair of streets — is Waterloo and Queen Streets, with their Catholic churches, Hindu temple, Chinese temple and Jewish synagogue. Here along these streets were enclaves of Portuguese Eurasians, Jewish, Chinese, Tamil and even an almost-forgotten Japanese community on the Middle Road side of the streets.

Specific places of worship that remain along these two streets include the Cathedral of the Good Shepherd (1847); St Joseph's Church (1912); the Church of Sts Peter and Paul (1870), which primarily served the Chinese Catholic community; the Church of our Lady of Lourdes (1888), which served the Tamil Catholic community; Maghain Aboth Synagogue (1878); the Kwan Im Thong Hood Cho Temple (first established 1884) and dedicated to the worship of the Goddess of Mercy (Kwan Im); Sri Krishnan Temple (1869), dedicated exclusively to the worship of Sri Krishnan; and the former Methodist Church (1875), transformed into an arts and cultural space today. The Central Sikh Temple was also built here in the 1930s, but it was pulled down to make way for housing developments in the 1980s.

The area just in front of the Kwan Im Thong Hood Cho and the Sri Krishnan Temples, which literally sit side by side, is a particularly bustling and unique pedestrian thoroughfare today, with thousands of pilgrims and worshippers thronging to pay their respects to the various deities enshrined within the two temples. In particular, Chinese worshippers are known to light joss-sticks and pray to the Hindu deities just next door.

Waterloo and Queen Streets sit in the larger Bras Basah area, which, for much of the late 1800s and early 1900s, was regarded as European Town. Here it was that most of the European and Eurasian places of worship, as well as the historic British and Catholic Schools, were located.

The historic school buildings that still stand are the Catholic and Convent schools, including St Joseph's Institution (built in 1867), the former Catholic High Primary and Secondary Schools (1951 and 1936 respectively), the Convent of the Holy Infant Jesus (1903) and St Anthony's Convent (1906). Notably, all of these schools sat on or just across from Waterloo and Queen Streets. Other schools that used to be in the vicinity include the Raffles Institution and the Raffles Girls' School (demolished) and the Anglo-Chinese High School (which is today's National Archives building).

Other significant places of worship in the area include St Andrew's Cathedral, Masjid Bencoolen (established 1874) on Bencoolen Street, Wesley Methodist Church (1907), the Tamil Methodist Church on Short

RIGHT: Nagore Durgha Shrine, Telok Ayer Street, late 19th century.

Street (established 1887), the Prinsep Street Methodist Church (1930), serving the Straits Chinese community, and the Orchard Road Presbyterian Church (1878) — making the Bras Basah area possibly one of the most culturally and religiously diverse areas in Singapore then and today.

Food Culture

No discussion on the diverse cultures and communities of Singapore can be complete without a mention of food. Food is at the very heart of Singaporean culture and heritage. Ask any Singaporean, and the first response to the question as to what is unique about Singapore, is its food. And yet, almost all the dishes that are considered quintessentially Singaporean today did not originate in Singapore, but arrived along with the waves and varieties of immigrants that came to find opportunity and a new home.

Food heritage is possibly the most colourful and exciting form of heritage in Singapore, particularly as there is so much of it, and each and every dish represents the full diversity of world cultures that share this tiny island. A fuller discussion on food requires a multi-volume encyclopaedia. Here, we present a few representative dishes and how each and every one of them is cross-cultural in nature, much like Singapore itself.

The first, and perhaps the most common Singaporean dish, is Hainanese Chicken Rice, which originated in the island of Hainan to the south of China, and was ostensibly brought to Singapore by Hainanese immigrants. The dish consists of so-called "white-cut chicken" (白斬雞), a form of steamed chicken common in Cantonese *siu mei* (燒味) or "roast meat" cuisine rather than Hainanese cuisine. It is eaten with Southeast Asian long-grain rice (often Thai long-grain) which has been cooked in chicken stock infused with

ginger, garlic and pandan leaf, a unique Malayan herb. The dish is typically accompanied by three condiments: viscous dark soy sauce, minced ginger in chicken stock, and a spicy red chilli sauce. The latter is certainly not Chinese in the least, but an essential condiment in Southeast Asian cuisines.

Another staple of Singaporean food is satay, or skewers of marinated meat, grilled or barbecued over an open charcoal fire, and accompanied with a spicy peanut sauce. While Singaporeans consider it another "national dish", satay actually originates in the streets of Java in the former Netherlands East Indies. It spread throughout the Malay Archipelago wherever there were Malay-speaking communities, and became a kind of archetypal "street" or "hawker" cuisine of the region. The form of satay itself is also not indigenous to Southeast Asia, having drawn reference from the Indian and Persian *kebab*, very likely brought to the region by Persian and North Indian traders.

Curry is a mainstay of Singaporean cuisine, with every single community having its own traditional recipes. The unique Fish Head Curry is a particular favourite, with different communities claiming the dish as their own. The Chinese and Peranakans have their Assam Fish Head Curry, a sour-spicy concoction cooked with coconut milk and tamarind. The Indians have their own South Indian Fish Head Curry which is almost exactly the same thing, and which has possible roots in Kerala, India, which is the only state in India that boasts a fish head curry dish. Recent news reports tell of an enterprising Little India restaurateur who, noting Chinese diners' predilection for fish heads, invented this rather eye-catching dish. Whatever the case may be, it has become one of the city-state's most popular offerings.

In the dessert category, Nonya Kueh Kueh take the cake in terms of sheer colour, variety and pan-Singaporean popularity. Kueh Kueh are a

Singapore Sweet Meat Seller

generic term for sweet cakes and pastries. While generally regarded as
Nyonya today, the cakes and pastries have mixed Malay, Portuguese, Dutch,
Indian and Chinese origins. There are more than a dozen different types of
cakes with a range of different names: the rainbow-coloured *kueh lapis*; the
green and white *kueh salat*; the coconut-stuffed *kueh dadar*; the *gula melaka*
stuffed glutinous rice balls called *ondeh ondeh*; the bright-red, auspicious
Chinese *ang ku kueh*; the coconut-dusted brown tablet-shaped *kueh kosui* …
and many more besides. They are eaten as desserts accompanying dinner, or
snacks at any time during the day, and they make perfect gifts for visits to
friends' and family members' houses.

The Sugee Cake is a classic of Singapore's Eurasian heritage, being a
kind of semolina-based cake with almonds, marzipan and the occasional
splash of brandy. It is served at christenings, weddings, birthdays and parties
of all kinds. The cake has Portuguese origins, and may have originated
in Portuguese Goa from whence it probably travelled, together with the
Portuguese community, to Malacca and to Singapore. Sugee cake is typically
served with a pot of English tea, adding another layer of cross-culturalism to
this one simple form.

Finally, speaking of tea, one of the most essential Singaporean must-
haves is *teh tarik* or "pulled tea". This is a rich, milk tea that is rendered
frothy and light through being literally "pulled" from one scalding hot kettle
to another. While generally believed to be Malay in origin, it actually comes
from India. Walking down the streets of Calcutta today, one will probably
be surprised to find that the modest cup of *chai* tea offered to you by one of
the many street vendors, is, in fact, an older variant on *teh tarik* and tastes
quite the same. The vendor himself even pulls the tea much the same way
the Indian tea-seller in Singapore has done for more than a century.

CHAPTER FOUR

ARTS & LEISURE

BHARATANATYAM AND KATHAKALI

"81. Madira: The Glance in which the middle of the eye is rolling, the ends of the eyes are thin, the eyes are bent, and the corners of the eyes are fully widened, is called madira (intoxicated). It is to be used in representing light intoxication."

The Natyasastra – A Treatise on Hindu Dramaturgy and
Histrionics, Chapter VIII, Verse 81. Ascribed to Bharata Muni.
Translated from Sanskrit by Manomohan Ghosh (1951)

*B*haratanatyam and *Kathakali* belong to the larger canon of Indian classical dances that originated in antiquity on the Subcontinent and made their way to the East Indies and Singapore alongside the Indian communities that travelled there. Both dance forms are representative of Southern India, specifically Tamil Nadu for the Bharatanatyam and Kerala for the Kathakali. As such, they hold a particularly privileged place amongst the Indians in Singapore, who primarily hailed from the South.

The Bharatanatyam is perhaps the most well-known of the Indian classical dances not only in Singapore but worldwide. It is the older of the two, being rooted in the theories of dance expounded in the 2nd-century BC Sanskrit treatise, the *Natya Shastra*.

Originally performed only in the Hindu temples of the South, a ban on the form by British colonials in the early 1900s, and the subsequent independence of India in 1947, saw the dance form emerge from the temples onto the stage.

While modern presentations of the dance may provide for multiple dancers on the same stage, the traditional form of the dance calls only for a solo female dancer, who is accompanied by an Indian classical music ensemble, performing the Carnatic (or Southern Indian) style of classical music characterised by a very strong focus on vocals.

The Bharatanatyam is at heart a kind of stylised dance-theatre, with the single performer re-enacting, through extremely precise and highly codified forms of choreography, scenes from the Indian Epics, the *Ramayana* and the *Mahabharata*.

OPPOSITE: A kathakali dancer in the virtuous pachcha (green) role at Kochi, India.

Every inch of the dancer's body, from her toes to the tips of her fingers to her facial expressions and the swivel of her eyes, is choreographed according to an established "list" of dance gestures (suggested at by the quote at the beginning of the chapter). Her every move is accompanied by a vocalist speaking traditional onomatopoeics of rhythm – "*ta ti ge ti … ta ti ge ti*"… and by the sonorous strains of the *sitar* and the percussive strike of the *tabla*. The result is a mesmerising display of movement and sound that is meant to provide the viewer with a glimpse of the divine.

Certainly, the Bharatanatyam is also an extremely suggestive form of dance. The single female performer is always clad in the best of saris, with gold jewellery on her neck, ears and nose, and bouquets of jasmine threaded into her long black hair, tied into a ponytail. Her facial gestures are remarkably eloquent, expressing joy, fear, anger, relief, courage, flirtation, intoxication and satiation.

This primordial link between movement, suggestiveness and divinity, and the religious roots of dance itself in Hindu culture, can be seen in sculptural representations of the Hindu God Shiva as the *Nataraja*, or Lord of the Dance. The most spectacular of these sculptures are those cast in bronze by the Chola Kings of the Tamil South in as early as the 12th century AD, once again underscoring the ancient roots of the Bharatanatyam there.

The Kathakali is a more recent sibling of the Bharatanatyam, having emerged in its current form in Kerala only in the 17th century; though it too traces its roots back to temple-centered dance forms in the early part of the first millennium.

Like the Bharatanatyam, the Kathakali is also a form of dance-theatre – a stylised re-enactment of the Hindu Epics. The emphasis is more on the theatre rather than on the dance; indeed, the Kathakali repertoire counts hundreds of specific theatrical plays written.

Kathakali performances are typically long and are traditionally performed from dusk till dawn. Kathakali is also performed by an ensemble,

RIGHT: In Bharatanatyam, choreographed hand and finger gestures, known as *mudras*, are used to communicate a wide range of ideas and actions, and to represent flowers, animals and objects.

rather than a single performer, with male performers playing both male
and female roles. The entire performance is accompanied by musicians,
percussionists and vocalists singing in Malayalee, the language of Kerala.
Contemporary theatre audiences might find aspects of the performance
familiar, from the setting of the stage with stage lights — a row of *vilakas*,
or brass lamps, in this case; to the introduction of the characters behind
the *tereshiela*, or a satin "stage" curtain; to the use of costumes and makeup
by the cast.

On the latter, Kathakali has quite easily the most elaborate costumes and
make-up of all Indian classical dances. A Kathakali display is a riotous feast
of colour, with the actors decked out in psychedelic make-up requiring hours
of preparation, and voluminous robes culminating in large hoop skirts. To
heighten the sense of drama, face masks and headgear are thrown into the
mix; and specific colours and forms of costumes and makeup pertain to very
specific heroic or villainous characters in the repertoire.

Underneath the masks, face makeup, headgear and heavy costumes, the
actors are still expected to perform complicated pieces of choreography, with
a focus on the face, the eyes and the hands. It is no wonder then that training
to be a Kathakali performer is extremely rigorous and follows a system of
martial arts-style exercises known as the *Kalari Pyattu*.

A full performance of Kathakali is an event in its own right, one which
would have drawn audiences from neighbouring villages in the Kerala
of old. In those days, hundreds of people gathered on the green to enjoy
this extravaganza of dance, music, theatre and song; a presentation on the
universal theme of good versus evil, demons battling deities, and the epic
struggle of humankind. Today, in Singapore local and visiting troupes
continue to entertain.

BATIK

"Coloured cottons (járit) are distinguished into lúri or lúri gíng'gang, those in which the yarn is dyed previously to weaving; and bátik, those which are dyed subsequently. The process of weaving the former is similar to that of the gingham, which it resembles, and need not therefore be detailed; but the latter, being peculiar to Java, may deserve a more particular description."

— Thomas Stamford Raffles, *The History of Java* (1817)

The origins of batik are shrouded in mystery, with some scholars suggesting Chinese origins, others Indian, and yet others African. What is generally accepted is that at least in the last millennium the undisputed home of batik, where as an art form it has attained unrivalled sophistication and variety, is the island of Java, in the midst of the vast Indonesian Archipelago.

Already in the 14th century, the intrepid Chinese traveller, Wang Dayuan, remarked upon his arrival in Java, of the existence of floral-patterned fabrics, the colours of which did not run upon being exposed to water. Some 400 years later, a certain Thomas Stamford Raffles would actually document the technique of making batik in his monumental tome, *The History of Java*, released in 1817.

The technique of batik is extremely intricate. In short, it involves design production on fabric through the use of a wax resist method. With a traditional spouted implement known as a *canting*, or a pre-made copper stamp known as a *cap* (pronounced "chop"), a batik artisan applies melted beeswax onto fabric that has been washed and boiled in water multiple times to remove all traces of chemicals, starches and other impurities that may interfere with the dying process.

Depending on the status of the buyer or commissioner, the wax is applied in a variety of appropriate traditional designs and motifs, then the fabric is soaked in a dye bath. Areas not covered by the wax soak up the dye, while the wax-covered parts of the fabric retain their original white or off-white colour. For each colour that has to be applied to the fabric, the entire process of wax resist dyeing has to be repeated. The result is a very fine and elaborate printed textile, the colours of which hold fast when soaked in hot water.

Motifs and patterns for batik vary by region, status and ethnicity of the artisan and/or the commissioner. Motifs associated with the Royal Courts of Java are generally considered to be the most ancient and traditional of all motifs. In particular, the *parang rusak* (or "broken blade") motif which consists of a range of diagonal patterns, most notably extremely stylised folded blades dancing around on a brown background, was forbidden to the masses, and reserved for nobility at the Courts of Surakarta and Yogyakarta.

OPPOSITE: Batik Hokokai, north coastal Java (Pekalongan), 1940s. This variety of batik emerged during the Japanese occupation of Java during World War II and combines Japanese and Javanese elements such as the chrysanthemum and the parang rusak.

Other Javanese classical designs often used highly stylised representations of mythical animals such as the *naga*, the *garuda*, the *pucuk rebung* (bamboo shoot) and *pohon hayat* (tree of life) motifs. Characters from the *wayang kulit* (or shadow puppet play) also recur with some frequency.

From the 1800s on, Indian chintz or printed cotton from Bengal began flooding global markets via Dutch and later British colonial trade networks. Chintz reached Java through the ports of Batavia and Soerabaja and was immediately a source of great interest due to its vibrant colour and elaborate designs. How exactly the Bengalis managed to print these elaborate floral patterns onto cotton was a mystery; certainly there were efforts to copy and incorporate many of these floral motifs into the batik repertoire.

The Dutch and the Chinese also got in on the act. An entire genre of Dutch Compagnie style batiks emerged in the 1800s and early 1900s, helmed by Dutch-Eurasians or Indische peoples living in Java. Typically, they depicted European style motifs or European scenes on fabric. In the meantime, Chinese Peranakans also developed a unique batik style that incorporated Chinese motifs like the phoenix and the peony.

RIGHT ABOVE: Creating batik, mid 20th century.

BELOW: Batik stamp, Java, early to mid 20th century.

Batik was rather prevalently used. King and commoner alike used batik as a form of dress, as did men and women, children and adults, Javanese, European and Chinese. Batik was most commonly made into *kain sarung* or *kain panjang*, the sarong being a tubular textile that was wrapped round the lower half of the human frame to form a kind of loose skirt; and the panjang being a longer sarong.

The Chinese Peranakans also used batik pieces as altar cloths or *tokwi* — elaborate pieces of fabric laid upon the ancestral altar in the family home. The Dutch Eurasians also used batik as a form of adornment for the family table.

The other most popular use of batik today arose in the 1950s and '60s. This is the advent of the so-called formal batik shirt, which is a variation on a loose fitting, Hawaiian style casual shirt made for the Tropics. These batik shirts are considered formal wear for men today across Indonesia, Malaysia and Singapore. Yet another popular use of batik was in the uniforms of the national airlines of the Malay-speaking world, particularly as sarong and kebaya for air hostesses, namely for Malaysian Airlines, Garuda Indonesia, and Singapore Airlines. One need only recall the iconic Singapore Girl, decked out in her blue and gold kebaya and sarong skirt that was designed by Parisian couturier Pierre Balmain in 1968.

CRICKET IN SINGAPORE

Cricket is perhaps the most quintessential of British sports, a game the British took with them everywhere they went in the Age of Empire. And thus, this stalwart of British heritage also became part of the heritage of many erstwhile colonies of the British Empire, particularly in India, Pakistan and Sri Lanka.

The history of cricket in Singapore is almost as old as the history of Singapore itself. As with many other cities in British India and the Far East, the colonial social scene revolved around clubs, of which there was a variety. For much of the 1800s these clubs were exclusively for men, and involved some form of sport; sport and sporting activity having been seen as character-forming and the best way to nurture strapping young men suited for empire.

RIGHT: The pavilion of the Singapore Cricket Club, 1880s.

Cricket was played in Singapore from the 1830s onwards, with regular Sunday cricket matches taking place on the Esplanade by the waterfront. But it wasn't until 1852 that the Singapore Cricket Club was established. The Cricket Club was the third oldest sport-related club in Singapore. The first was the Singapore Yacht Club, established in 1826, followed by the Singapore Sporting Club, later the Turf Club in 1843.

From the beginning, the clubhouse was located on the south end of the Esplanade (today's Padang). This was a natural location not just because the Esplanade was also regarded as the fledgling colony's sporting green; but also because, situated by the commercial heart of Raffles Place, where many of its members worked, the clubhouse was a convenient place for luncheons and entertaining.

The original clubhouse was a mere wooden pavilion, built in the 1860s. This soon proved to be inadequate, so the second version of the clubhouse in the form of a colonial bungalow was erected in 1877. This also quickly proved to be too small, and so in 1884, the third and final version of the clubhouse was built. Further expansions, including the north and south wings of the building, were made in 1907 and 1922. The clubhouse, as it stands today at its Connaught Drive address, is the outcome of the final 1922 refurbishment.

In the beginning, the club had 28 members, mostly middle-class men working in junior positions at the merchant and trading houses in the colony. These would have been the same men that had been playing cricket on the Esplanade. By the 1880s, however, membership had grown to almost 400 with some of the most powerful gentlemen in the colony — heads of businesses and senior government officials — being members. Thus, the Singapore Cricket Club became one of the most premier and exclusive clubs in the colony, second only to the Singapore Club (established in 1862, and later to be the Singapore Town Club).

Membership of the club was limited to Europeans only, and this riled other communities in town, notably the Eurasians, who established their own Singapore Recreation Club — initially also a cricket club — at the northern end of the Esplanade in 1883, right across from the Singapore Cricket Club. Meanwhile, the wealthy Straits Chinese community established their own sporting club, the Singapore Chinese Recreational Club at Hong Lim Green in 1885.

Cricket matches and tournaments were held annually on the Padang. The cream of society, men and women alike, decked out in their best suits and dresses, gathered at the main pavilion of the Cricket Club to watch the tournament as it unfolded on the green. The players, decked out in their cricket whites (all-white light shirt and trouser ensembles) played in accordance with rules set down more than 200 years earlier. During each inning, the bowler tossed the ball to the batsman, while the umpires watched at each end of the pitch. The goal of the game is for the batting team to score more runs, and the bowling team to prevent them from doing so.

Cricket in Singapore took a hit during the War, and it never quite recovered in the aftermath of the colonial era, particularly due to the advent of other sports like hockey, football and rugby, all of which grew in popularity. Where cricket still has a strong following today is in the United Kingdom, of course, but also in Australia, New Zealand and in the former British Raj — today's India, Pakistan and Bangladesh. That said, the Singapore Cricket Club still has the occasional cricket match on the Padang, and cricket is played elsewhere in Singapore such as on the grounds of the Ceylon Sports Club. There is also a national team fielded by the Singapore Cricket Association.

Chinese Wayang

Chinese wayang, or simply *wayang*, is the local name for Chinese Street Opera, which arrived by the mid-1800s in Singapore, by way of the many Chinese immigrant communities. The word "wayang" is Malay for an outdoor dramatic performance.

Chinese Street Opera was mass audience entertainment in its time. In the absence of any other form of entertainment, wayang was perhaps the most widespread and popular art form for the immigrant Chinese community, with many a performance taking place each night on hastily put-together stages starring amateur performers and musicians. The earliest record of a Chinese opera performance organised on the streets dates to 1842.

RIGHT: Chinese wayang performance, c. 1905.

RIGHT: Characters from Chinese opera: dan, or female character (left); sheng, or male character (right). Early 21st century.

Like Indian classical dance, there are many regional variants of Chinese opera, but three main southern forms have been most popular in Singapore, on account of their catering to the three largest Chinese dialect groups here. These were Cantonese Opera, Teochew Opera, and Hokkien Opera.

All three forms had similarities, in that they involved heavily made-up performers — primarily male though eventually women joined the stage — in elaborately embroidered costumes. Performing song and stylised dramatic numbers, they also incorporated mime, acrobatics, martial arts and dance. There were subtle differences in the style of makeup and costumes, but the primary difference was in the dialect in which the repertoire was performed.

This repertoire was rich indeed, including a wide variety of Chinese myths, legends and morality tales, or episodes from Chinese epics like *The Water Margin*, *Generals of the Yang Family*, *Journey to the West* or *The Romance of the Three Kingdoms*.

Performances often lasted through the night. And as the performers performed on stage, audiences would sip tea and snack as they enjoyed the comedic or dramatic theatrics. Originally, these performances were held on temple grounds for the enjoyment of deities and spirits during popular festivals and birthdays of deities, and in particular, during the Seventh-month Ghost Festival when the gates of hell opened, and the spirits returned to earth for entertainment. Later, performances moved out into the streets themselves.

A Chinese street opera performance is a boisterous and pretty loud affair. The music and dramatics can be heard for miles around — which is the exact intent — for performing troupes naturally wish to maximise the number of audiences they can attract at any one evening.

The specific roles in a Chinese opera are fixed: there is the *sheng*, the male protagonist; the *dan*, or female protagonist, typically played by a man until very recently; the *chou*, or the male clown; and the *jing*, a secondary male character. Each of these is further subcategorised into other characters like the *laosheng*, an old, dignified male character, and *xiaosheng*, a younger male character. These character types are standard fare for all forms of Chinese opera, even northern older variants like Peking Opera and Kunqu.

Chinese opera performances are also typically accompanied by a traditional Chinese music ensemble with instruments including an *erhu* or two-stringed fiddle, lutes like the *yangqin* and *pipa*, woodwinds like *dizi* and *houguan*, a particularly strident trumpet-like instrument known as the *suona* and various percussive instruments such as drums, cymbals and clappers, or *bangzi*.

As wayang became more and more popular, purpose-made theatres were built, primarily in the Chinatown area. These often doubled up as teahouses, where patrons could enjoy a Chinese opera performance while sipping tea and entertaining clients or friends and family. A particularly famous Chinese opera teahouse in its time was the Lai Chun Yuen (黎春園) on Smith Street in Chinatown. Built in 1887, it was one of the most popular haunts at the turn of the 19th century, and still stands today, albeit transformed into a boutique hotel.

With the passage of time and the emergence of other contemporary forms of mass entertainment such as music and television, wayang has faded significantly in terms of popularity, though it has not died out. A handful of professional and semi-professional troupes still perform regularly in Singapore, although largely within the confines of professional theatres rather than on the street.

When one still has the opportunity to experience a traditional Chinese wayang is during the Seventh Month Ghost festival, when troupes are allowed to put up makeshift street theatres and perform their repertoire for eager guests, both human and incorporeal. Even then, however, a rather more contemporary form of music inspired by opera and Chinese pop music, and known generically as *getai* (歌台), has taken over in popularity and is more likely to be witnessed than Chinese wayang per se.

THE CUSTOM OF SIREH

The custom of chewing sireh, or betel, is an ancient one, having been practised for more than 1,000 years. It is widespread in Asia, with almost all countries of South and Southeast Asia, including Southern China and Taiwan, having once practised or is still practising this custom regularly. Sireh is the Malay-Indonesian name for betel. Elsewhere in Asia, it goes by a different name: *paan* in Hindi, *vettrilai* in Tamil, *kwun-ya* in Burmese, *mahk* in Thai, and *bin-lang* (檳榔) in Chinese.

RIGHT: Tepak Sireh,
Surabaya, 19th century.

The word "sireh" itself refers to the betel leaf, which belongs to a kind of vine that grows all over South and Southeast Asia. The sireh is chewed with the *pinang* or areca nut, also a native of South and Southeast Asia. Slices or small chunks of pinang are folded carefully in a sireh leaf and enhanced in flavour with cloves, a dash of slaked lime and occasionally, tobacco. The resulting quid is then popped into one's mouth and chewed.

As with its name, the manner in which the pinang is folded into the sireh leaf varies with geography and can be very elaborate indeed. However the sireh is taken and chewed, the effects of chewing are the same — a kind of mild buzz or mini-high, due to the betel leaf being a form of psycho-active stimulant. The chewing of the sireh induces salivation, and saliva, when mixed with the chewed pulp of the areca nut, turns a distinctive bright red. After chewing, the bright red remains of the sireh are spat out.

In the Malay Archipelago, sireh was chewed by royalty and common folk, rich and poor alike, and an elaborate ritual evolved that accompanied the act of preparing and chewing sireh. The different parts of the sireh — leaf, nut, spice, lime and tobacco — were often housed in an elaborate container known as a *tepak sireh* or "sireh box". The word "box" belies the fact that these tepak sireh were often exquisite works of art in their own right, made in a variety of materials and styles: some were made in pure silver, some with valuable woods inlaid with mother-of-pearl, others in teak and overlaid with silver and gold.

Within the tepak sireh, each of the components has its equally elaborate container. Leaves are stored in a fan-shaped receptacle known as a *bekas sireh*, the nut and spices in various small containers called *combol-combol*, and there is also an elaborately made *kacip* or areca-nut cutter, and a *gobek* or pestle and mortar to crush the nut before consuming it. No tepak sireh set is complete without the accompanying *ketur*, or spittoon; these can be equally elaborately made, often in silver, enamel or porcelain.

Sireh-chewing was intricately linked with the custom of hospitality in the Malay World. When a visitor paid a visit to one's home, it was customary to offer him or her a quid of betel to chew. The host, or more often the hostess, prepared the quid using the implements in her elaborately made tepak sireh, then offered the quid to her guest and made one for herself. After the quid was chewed, they used the spittoon for the remains.

Sireh was adopted as a custom by all ethnicities in the Malay World, not just the Malays and Indonesians, but also the Baba-Nyonya, the Eurasians and the Europeans themselves. For example, for much of the history of the Netherlands East Indies, the Dutch-Eurasian or Indische families also practised the custom of sireh, making it an almost universal aspect of living in the Malay World.

Unfortunately, prolonged chewing of sireh was unhealthy and resulted in teeth stained black by the corrosive mix of the areca nut juice and saliva. Recent health studies have also revealed that sireh itself is carcinogenic and the cause for high instances of mouth and other oral cancers everywhere it is chewed. It is no longer a practice in Singapore and only the tepak sireh remains — frequently collected as an exquisite work of art. Elsewhere, however, large amounts are still chewed and consumed every day in outright ignorance of its dangerous health effects.

JAWI

Before the Malay language was written in Latin script, it was written in a modified version of the Arabic alphabet. This was known as *jawi*, after *Jawah*, the Arabic name for Java, which was a reference to the entire Malay Archipelago.

The exact point at which jawi was adopted as the official script of Classical Malay and thus the Malay World is not clear, but it almost certainly arrived with Islam. Certainly, by the time of the Sultanate of Malacca in 1400 AD, jawi was already in widespread use, being the official script of the Royal Courts and of classical Malay literature. The Malay epics — the likes of the *Sejarah Melayu* and the *Hikayat Hang Tuah*; classical Malay odes and *pantuns* (love songs), Sufi treatises, and familiar fables and tales, were written in jawi.

The use of jawi tied the Malay World closely to the lands of Islam, since the Arabic script was the script of the Qur'an, the holy book of the Muslims. Other Islamic cultures like the Persians, the Mughals and the Ottoman Turks had also adopted a modified version of the Arabic script for their own languages upon their conversion to Islam, and indeed Farsi and Urdu are still written today with the Arabic alphabet. The use of the Arabic

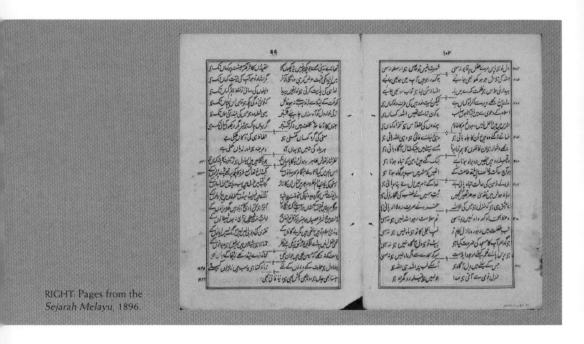

RIGHT: Pages from the
Sejarah Melayu, 1896.

script ostensibly allowed for easier access to the language of the Qur'an, and thus for a closer relationship between the worshipper and the religion.

Because the spoken Arabic language and spoken Malay are different, six new characters had to be created in the jawi alphabet to represent sounds that Arabic did not have, specifically the "ch", "p", "g" (as in get), "ng" (as in goiNG), "v" and "ny" (as in meNU). Conversely, there were certain sounds in Arabic, in particular gutturals and glottal stops, that were rarely enunciated in Malay.

Like Arabic, however, jawi is also written from right to left, and it is essentially an alphabetic script, rather than an ideographic script (like Chinese). Being fundamentally Arabic, jawi also lent itself to calligraphy and the calligraphic arts; and books written in jawi are often regarded as works of art in their own right. Certainly, a familiarity with jawi allowed the calligrapher-artist to create beautifully stylised calligraphic works based on Koranic surahs or pieces of Sufi poetry.

While jawi was never formally abolished as such, it was eventually eclipsed by the Latin alphabet, known as *rumi* in reference to Rum, the Arabic name for Rome.

Rumi was officially introduced by the Dutch in the former Netherlands East Indies in the early 1900s. The orthographic script invented in the Netherlands East Indies was called the Von Ophuijsen Spelling system after Charles von Ophuijsen, who based the script on Dutch orthography. He introduced it in 1901 and it was then used to teach Malay in schools, in order to have the Malay language more easily understood by the Dutch colonials.

By 1904, the lands of British Malaya and Borneo had their own officially version of Latin script, based on the English system of orthography. This script was known as the Wilkinson Spelling system script, after its creator, Richard James Wilkinson.

Numerous reforms of the rumi spelling systems took place separately in Malaysia and Indonesia in the course of the 1900s. In 1972, a common spelling system was finally introduced across Indonesia, Malaysia and Singapore. Jawi is still used occasionally in the Malay world, however, with Brunei maintaining it as an official script alongside rumi.

In Singapore, one occasionally still finds signs in the four national languages (English, Chinese, Malay and Tamil) with Malay written in jawi, a nostalgic reminder of the past. That said, interest in jawi is once again resurging, with many young Singaporeans learning the script.

THE KERIS

Of all the aspects of the Malay World's culture and heritage, none is more fraught with mystery and import than that of the *keris*. By definition, a keris is simply a traditional Malay-style dagger with a wavy blade. But its form, purpose and meaning defy this simple description; and the keris itself is at the core of ritual, tradition and ceremony.

The origins of the keris are steeped in superstition and mystery. Some say that the style of weaponry originated in India and was brought over by Hindu seafarers in antiquity. Certainly, the earliest known records of keris-making date from the Majapahit era, the Majapahit Empire being a thoroughly Hindu-ised Empire that ruled Java, Sumatra, the Malay Peninsula and much of the Malay World as it is known today.

A keris consists of three parts. The first, and the most important, is the blade (or *bilah* in Malay). This blade is typically wavy, and the number of waves, or *lok*, can range from three to more than 30. Given the pre-Islamic provenance of the keris itself, it is widely believed that the wavy form of the blade resembles that of a naga or dragon in Malay-Javanese mythology. Not all keris are necessarily wavy — as a rule, the more ceremonial the keris, the more waves it has; traditional executioner's or warrior's keris were generally straight.

Most keris are damascened, in that they sport a pattern on the blade that is a result of the use of two or more different metals in the blade's forging. The Malay term for the pattern is *pamor*, and an elaborately patterned blade is often known as *berpamor*. The pattern itself may have symbolic or ritual meaning, and is often talismanic, bestowing a kind of good luck or warrior's strength to the wielder.

The blade is also asymmetric with the side of the blade closer to the hilt having an elaborate silhouette which some say recalls the silhouette of an

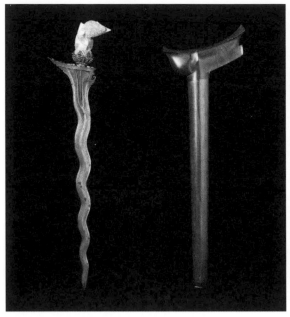

elephant with its trunk (the name of these features is *gajah*, or elephant); others argue that the silhouette may be a stylised human face, that, with the advent of Islam, was gradually rendered abstract due to Islam's prohibition of human figural representation.

The second important part of the keris is the hilt, or *hulu*. This hooked or L-shaped hilt is the means by which one determines the style of the keris, of which there are many. The Balinese and Javanese styles, having a direct lineage to ancient Majapahit styles, often have extremely elaborate figural hilts. The Balinese, in particular, depict their Hindu deities and demons on hilts. Conversely, the Malay, Bugis and Sumatran keris often sport far more stylised and abstract hilts, recalling the form of deities and demons, but without the features.

Unlike the dagger or the rapier, which the keris resembles, the hilt and dagger are designed in a way that has the wielder grasp the L-shaped hilt in his palm and thrust the keris forward in a way that is extremely lethal. The blade being curved and often also extremely sharp, it is impossible for a keris to leave a victim's body without doing extensive bodily harm.

Finally, the third part of the keris is the sheathe, which is T-shaped and also has regional variants, the Bugis and Javanese sheathes resembling the form of sailing vessels, and the Malay sheathes being far more simple T-shapes. Sheathes are most often made of wood and the choosing of the wood also involves an elaborate process of deciding the right kind of tree from which to retrieve the wood. The spirit energy, or *semangat*, of the tree, will imbue the sheathe and the keris with the appropriate warrior's strength or luck.

All cultures that wield the keris believe that each keris has a spirit energy, or semangat within it. The semangat is bestowed on and accumulated in the keris through a few avenues: through the process of forging itself, when the forger could, in the course of forging, choose the right kinds of metal to give form to the right kinds of pamor; through the carving of the hilt and sheathe, which bestows the keris a certain character and personality; and through the choice of the wood itself, as mentioned earlier.

Keris were used widely by commoners, warriors and royalty alike, with the more elaborately carved being more suited to royalty. Where for centuries the keris was a weapon through and through, the advent of firearms and the discouragement of weapons by colonial authorities in the 19th century resulted in the decline of the use of the keris as a weapon. Keris have since taken on more of a ceremonial role, often borne by men as a means of declaring their social status.

In Malay folklore and mythology, there have been a few famous keris. Perhaps the most famous is the *Taming Sari*, a magic keris which could disguise itself in other forms, and which was used by the legendary Malay warrior Hang Tuah, who lived in the 1400s in Malacca during the Malacca Sultanate. The story of Hang Tuah and Taming Sari is recounted in a fabulously swashbuckling epic known as the *Hikayat Hang Tuah*. Taming Sari, itself, was a straight blade and it was purportedly handed down through generations, remaining today in the Royal Regalia of the Perak Royal Family.

In Singapore, the keris is largely seen as a ceremonial object, endowing the bearer with a specific social status. It is also collected as a work of art in its own right — a symbol of traditional Malay culture and heritage that developed indigenously in the Malay World.

The Lion Dance and the Dragon Dance

On festive occasions, primarily during the Chinese New Year, the streets of Singapore, and other major centres of Chinese diaspora communities in Southeast Asia, come alive with various forms of festivities, two of the most eye-catching being the Lion Dance and the Dragon Dance.

With roots dating back to the Han Dynasty (turn of the 1st millennium), both dances are an integral part of Chinese culture. The Lion Dance is prevalent throughout East Asia, in Japan, Korea and Vietnam. In China, there are two main variants: the Northern Lion, which originated in the Central Plains, and the Southern Lion, which originated in the Cantonese heartlands.

In Southeast Asia, including Singapore, the Southern Lion predominates, as the Chinese diaspora communities came largely from Southern China. The form of the Southern Lion is rather more stylised than its northern counterpart, and looks less like an actual lion. It is primarily distinguished by its large lion's head made from papier maché which has highly expressive eyes and mouth, both of which flap and move. The head is often attached to a cape-like fabric that functions as the lion's body, and is draped over the dancers that wield the lion. Two dancers are required for each lion: one carries and manipulates the head as one would manipulate a ventriloquist's puppet, while the other functions as the lion's lower half. The dancers wear stylised pants meant to evoke the lion's four legs.

Because of the weight of the lion's head and the dexterousness of the dance steps, performing the Lion Dance can be an extremely exhausting and gruelling affair. Lion dancers are thus trained in Chinese Martial Arts or *wushu*, in order to build strength, stamina and flexibility. Trainees are apprenticed to seasoned masters in order to learn the tricks of the trade, with individual performing troupes typically boasting their own distinctive moves or repertoires. A Lion Dance is further accompanied by a percussion ensemble consisting of a variety of large drums and cymbals, all intent on creating as much noise as possible in order to create a general environment of buzz and boisterousness — what the Chinese value as *re nao* (熱鬧).

During the Chinese New Year, the Lion Dance is used to "chase away" the old Year; in Chinese mythology, the year or *nian* was literally represented as a ferocious monster, and some say the Southern Chinese Lion may actually be a modification of the Year beast. Aside from the Chinese New Year, Lion Dances are also commissioned as a form of blessing and good luck for other occasions such as the opening of new businesses, for auspicious festive days and for birthdays.

RIGHT: Lion dance, Singapore, c. 1950s.

RIGHT: Dragon dance, Singapore, c. 1950s.

The Dragon Dance is most often performed during the Chinese New Year Season, particularly since it is a far more elaborate form of performance. Like the Southern Lion, the distinguishing feature of the Dragon Dance is the large head of the dragon, which is made from papier maché and is painted in extremely vivid colours and with very life-like features.

The body of the dragon is made through joining a series of lightweight hoops with paper or fabric. The body is segmented, with each segment of the body being carried by one performer with a pole stuck to the segment. The dragon's body can be anything between 25 and 50 metres in length, requiring some dozen to two dozen performers each carrying a segment of the beast, with one carrying the head and the tail respectively.

Like lion dancers, performers of the dragon dance are also grounded in wushu, in order to build strength and stamina for often very demanding performances. Unlike lion dances, which are commissioned for specific locations, dragon dances are often performed as part of larger processions, so a performance may last for hours on end.

The dragon moves in waves and some typical tricks involve it spiraling and corkscrewing as though it were swimming in water or flying through the air. In early China, dragons were intimately linked to water and the seas — in particular the Dragon Kings of the Seas — and dragon dances were used as rain dances, literally to pray for the arrival of life-giving rains. In later years, the dragon's appearance became linked to that of the Emperor, and the dragon dance was a show of divine authority, imperial might and imperial benevolence and largesse. Today, dragon dances have lost their ancient symbolic meaning, but they are still commissioned as a form of good luck; to herald a good harvest; and as a way to keep alive ancient cultural traditions.

Beyond East Asia and Southeast Asia, the Lion and Dragon Dances have also gone global, alongside the Chinese diasporas worldwide.

"Then at the suggestion of the vulture Sampati, the mighty Hanuman crossed the salt sea extending for a hundred yojanas. And arriving at the city of Lanka, ruled by Ravana, he found Sita in the midst of an Asoka wood, absorbed in thought. And then having shown her the sign, he related unto her all about the friendship between Rama and Sugriva, and having cheered Videha's daughter, he smashed the gate of the palace."

— *The Ramayana*, Book 1

The *Ramayana* is the great national epic of India — and of the many Southeast Asian civilisations that have been touched by India in the course of their history. No discussion of heritage in Singapore can be without a section on the *Ramayana*, not least because Singapore sits in the very middle of Southeast Asia, and because the *Ramayana* has had a long and pervasive influence on many aspects of Southeast Asian arts whether it be literature, theatre, performance or visual art.

The epic is thought to have been authored by the poet-sage, Valmiki, and completed sometime in the 5th century BC. It is perhaps the largest epic of world literature, consisting of more than 20,000 verses and close to half a million words. It was originally written in Sanskrit, though it has since been translated into many languages.

The basic narrative of the *Ramayana* is that of a hero's quest, as well as the universal tale of good triumphing over evil. The protagonist, Prince Rama of the ancient Kingdom of Ayodhya, has his wife, Sita, abducted by the Demon-King Ravana. Over the course of many battles and journeying, and with the help of his brother Lakshmana, as well as other semi-divine beings, the most notable being Hanuman, the Monkey-God, Rama plucks Sita from Ravana's clutches and the couple live happily ever after.

BELOW: Leaf from the *Ramayana*, Maharashtra or Tamil Nadu, Maratha Period (18th century).

RIGHT: Hanuman, Myanmar, 19th century.

This is, of course, a very simplified re-telling of the tale. The full version of the tale is far more dramatic and swashbuckling, involving swords, spears, maces and magic arrows; garudas, green ogres, whales, white elephants and other strange beasts; and the involvement of an entire pantheon of colourful and characterful deities, demi-gods and demons. The stirring and unforgettable nature of the *Ramayana* has contributed to its longevity in the Indian and Southeast Asian worlds.

The *Ramayana* first travelled to Southeast Asia in the early centuries of the first millennium AD when Hinduism was adopted as the official religion for the many great kingdoms of mainland as well as maritime Southeast Asia. The Kingdom of Angkor, certainly, but also the city-states of the Pyu in Myanmar, the Cham in lower Indochina, and the Majapahit Empire are all included here.

Hinduism was gradually eclipsed as a state religion first by Buddhism when it swept through at the turn of 10th century, and subsequently — in maritime Southeast Asia, at least — by Islam in the 14th century. But some aspects of Hindu culture were not completely eradicated and still remain even today. They co-exist alongside the official religions of Buddhism in mainland Southeast Asia and Islam in maritime Southeast Asia, and have given rise to some hybrid forms of art.

In particular, the *Ramayana*, being a universal tale of good over evil, love and betrayal, held tremendous staying power across Southeast Asia, with many nations adopting it, or at least versions of it, as their so-called

RIGHT: Relief from Borobudur, Central Java, 1893.

BELOW: Wayang kulit shadow puppet figures of Semar (top) and Hanuman (below), Java, 20th century.

"National Epic". In Thailand, the *Ramayana* is known as the *Ramakien*, and its most thrilling expression is found in the splendid *Ramakien* murals that adorn the inner cloister walls of the Grand Palace in Bangkok. Similarly, Cambodian *Reamker* murals adorn the walls of the Royal Palace in Phnom Penh. Elsewhere, the Burmese have their *Yama Zatdaw*, the Lao *Phra Lak Phra Lam*, the Javanese *Kakawin Ramayana*, the Balinese *Ramakavaca*, and the Malays *Hikayat Seri Rama*.

In all these lands, the *Ramayana* persists today in the form of elaborate dance and theatrical forms that present specific tales from the epic. All the countries mentioned above still retain a tradition of courtly dances that are representations of the various exploits and achievements of Rama, Sita and in particular, Hanuman. These dances involve elaborate choreography and costumes, and often utilise intricately carved masks.

In Java and the Malay World, another popular form of presenting the *Ramayana* emerged in the form of *wayang kulit*, or shadow puppet theatre. Here, extremely stylised puppets, often made of animal hide, are used to tell the tale of Rama and Sita to enraptured audiences.

In Indonesia, Malaysia and Singapore, in the old days at least, wayang kulit troupes would ply the streets at festival seasons, and regale gathered revelers with comic and tragic antics. These troupes, performing in hastily made theatres accompanied by singers and musicians, often performed through the night to spellbound audiences.

Sarong Kebaya

"In their houses, they generally go about with undressed hair and bareheaded, and wear a blouse called baju, which comes down over the navel and is so sheer that the whole body can be seen. From the navel down they simply wear a painted cloth wrapped three or four times around the body. These cloths are very beautifully made and rather costly, with many figures and woven work of various colours. Furthermore, the rest of the body is naked, without anything worn over the legs or feet; bare feet are placed in mules or slippers, like those of the men..."

— Jan Huygen van Linschoten, *Itinerario* (1596)

Sarong kebaya is lady's formal dress in the Malay World, equivalent to the evening gown for Westerners, the kimono for Japanese ladies or the cheongsam for Chinese ladies. It is a remarkably sensual yet efficient form of skirt-blouse ensemble, its loose and light nature entirely adapted to the Tropics, and its close-fitting, shapely form accentuating a lady's curves.

The sarong refers to the skirt of the ensemble and is actually a misnomer coined by the English. The actual Malay term for the skirt is the *kain*, which refers to a long, printed fabric, typically batik or other styles of printed fabric like *ikat* or *songket*. This fabric is unstitched and typically wrapped and folded tightly around the waist to form the skirt.

The kebaya refers to the long-sleeved blouse, which is often made of a sheer fabric such as silk, in white or other colours, and embellished with lace and embroidery. While today the blouse may be fastened at the front with buttons, traditionally the blouse was typically fastened with a row of jewelled brooches, known as kerongsang. The kebaya, like the cheongsam, is body hugging and has to be tailored to the form of the lady. In the traditional Javanese sarong kebaya, the kebaya is often worn with a *kemban*, or torso wrap to preserve modesty.

Sarong kebaya as it appears today is a hybrid form that emerged in the Asian port cities of the Portuguese Empire in the 1500s. Its origins lie in the Majapahit Empire in Java, where a variation on the sarong kebaya ensemble was a form of courtly dress that only queens and princesses would wear.

The Portuguese first encountered the sarong when they conquered Malacca in 1511. Being primarily men, they inter-married with local Malay women in their initial years of colonisation, and generations of their Eurasian children adopted some of the Malay customs and traditions of their mothers. This included customs such as chewing betel, speaking Malay and wearing the sarong.

RIGHT: Nyonya ladies in sarong kebaya: (left) Straits Settlements or Indonesia, 1910s–1920s; (right) Straits Settlements or Indonesia, 1940s–1950s.

The use of the sarong was deemed so comfortable that the Portuguese brought this indigenous Malay dress with them to other colonies in Asia — to Goa, Macao and even as far afield as Nagasaki. The kebaya as it appears today, is probably a variation on the traditional Portuguese lace blouse and mantilla, which Portuguese-Eurasian ladies donned in combination with their sarong.

The resulting sarong kebaya proved to have an enduring impact on women's dress in Southeast Asia. When the Dutch took over the Portuguese in Java and Malacca, they simply took over from where the Portuguese left off, their menfolk similarly marrying local Malay and Portuguese Eurasian ladies, and their women and children adopting the customs of the mother, including wearing sarong kebaya, chewing betel and speaking Malay.

The tradition continued even after the British came through Southeast Asia. The British had been scandalised by the use of the sarong, which they came to view as a kind of pyjama, and by the dark-skinned Eurasian ladies who considered themselves Dutch but sat on the floor with their servants and chewed betel continuously. They tried to eradicate many of these localised customs, but failed.

In the meantime, of course, Malay women and women of other races in the port cities also took to wearing sarong kebaya as a popular dress. In fact, sarong kebaya became so widespread and so popular by the late 1800s that it was deemed fashionable and de rigeur for all ladies to own one. Malay and Javanese royalty were seen sporting sarong kebaya; so too the wealthy Nyonya, or Straits Chinese ladies, who evolved their own style of sarong kebaya with auspicious Chinese motifs printed in batik and accompanying kasut manek, or beaded slippers.

Up until the 1960s, celebrities and film stars regularly wore sarong kebaya and batik print makers and kebaya tailors alike ran bustling businesses. The sarong kebaya was adopted as national dress in Indonesia and unofficial national dress in Malaysia and Singapore. All three national carriers — Garudu Indonesia, Malaysian Airlines and Singapore Airlines — adopted the sarong kebaya as their uniform, with the Singapore Girl in her sarong kebaya being perhaps the most easily recognisable airline icon worldwide.

With growing Islamisation of Malay culture, many Malay women have abandoned the sarong kebaya for the more conservative and loose-fitting *baju panjang* and *baju kurong*, leaving only Straits Chinese women to continue the tradition of wearing sarong kebaya — and in fact adopting it as part of their unique identity. This has resulted in the mistaken impression that sarong kebaya is the reserve of the Straits Chinese alone.

THE TANG SHIPWRECK COLLECTION

The Tang Shipwreck Collection is perhaps the most significant collection of treasures in Singapore's National Collection — its store of moveable heritage. A generous gift from the Estate of Khoo Teck Puat, the patriarch of a pioneering Singaporean family, it now sits in a dedicated permanent gallery at the Asian Civilisations Museum. But for more than 1,000 years, it sat at the bottom of the sea.

The Tang Shipwreck consists of some 60,000 pieces of ceramics, gold, silver and other luxury and everyday goods from the 9th century, found in a sunken ship off Belitung Island, off the southeastern shore of Sumatra. The ship was an Omani dhow taking its precious cargo from the port city of Canton — the largest port city of Tang China, and quite possibly the world — westward to the port city of Basra in present-day Iraq, where it was bound for Baghdad, the capital city of the Abbasid Caliphate. As it rounded the tip of Peninsula Malaya (where Singapore is today), it somehow got blown off course, and crashed in the reefs and shallow waters off Belitung Island.

The presence of the ship and its cargo proves without a doubt that alongside the overland silk route between Tang Dynasty China and the Abbasid Caliphate, there was also a thriving maritime silk route taking luxury goods and spices from the East to the cities of the Middle East and onwards to Byzantium and the West.

The vast majority of the cargo — some 50,000 odd pieces — consisted of Changsha bowls, simple everyday brown stoneware so-called because they were fired in the Changsha kilns in today's Hunan province. They weren't luxury goods in the least; in China, they were used for tea drinking, though it isn't clear what their use would have been in the Arab world. Their significance lies in their demonstrating how the Chinese were already

producing ceramics for export on an industrial scale in the 9th century. Each and every piece of Changsha ware was fired by hand with motifs that catered to Arab taste: no single bowl is exactly the same.

The ship contained other wares catering to the Arab export market — including green splashware (the contemporary of *tang san cai*, or Tang Tricolour splashware), whiteware, and blue-and-white ware. Most notably, the three intact pieces of blue-and-white ware are the earliest intact blue-and-whites found anywhere in the world. They too had been produced for the Islamic market, and it would be some 400 years later, during the Yuan Dynasty, that China would mass-produce blue-and-white ware once again for export.

Alongside the Changsha bowls and ceramics sat a rather unique piece — a treasure amongst treasures. This is a tall green-splash wine ewer, made in the shape of a dragon. Its form is clearly not Chinese at all, but Sasanian Persian, demonstrating yet again how ingenious the Chinese were at catering to foreign taste. Though it was made in the shape of a wine ewer, it would have most likely been ornamental, since the handle of the ewer is too fine to have held the weight of a full vessel. This was clearly a commission, an order made by a wealthy merchant, possibly, who would have been content to wait a good two years before he would receive his order. Sadly, the order would never arrive.

Near the dragon ewer in the Tang Shipwreck Gallery of the Asian Civilisations Museum is displayed another group of exquisite pieces amongst the treasures. These are some half a dozen solid gold items, including dishes with wild geese motifs and early depictions of Buddhist swastikas (Tang China was a Buddhist Dynasty). The centrepiece of this display is a gold wine cup. The form of the cup, once again, is foreign; it is octagonal and possibly derives from Central Asian forms. Around the cup are depicted musicians at the Royal Court. What is interesting about these musicians is that none of them are Chinese. Rather they comprise of a variety of Central Asian and Western races — Persian, Sogdian, Syrian, Bactrian. They are a testament to the cosmopolitan, multi-cultural nature of the Tang Empire, and in particular, its capital city Chang-an.

In spirit, this cosmopolitanism and multi-culturalism resonates with Singapore today, where this precious cargo has found its permanent home.

THE NANYANG STYLE — MODERN ART IN SINGAPORE

The turn of the 19th century was characterised by the emergence of Modern Art as a movement worldwide. By its very nature, "modern" art called for the repudiation of traditional forms of representative and figural art — traditional "ways of seeing", in other words — for far more radical and experimental techniques of representation.

The late 19th century saw the Impressionists — Monet, Manet, Seurat, Van Gogh — experiment with light and colour in the depiction of landscapes and scenes of everyday life. The Interwar years saw the Cubists and Surrealists take the stage, led by Pablo Picasso and Salvador Dali respectively. The early 20th century saw the Expressionists — Pollock, Rothko, Twombly, De Kooning — toy with abstraction and dynamism as ends in themselves.

In Singapore, the mid-20th century saw the emergence of the Nanyang Style of painting. "Nanyang" translates as "Southern Seas"; it was the Chinese name for Southeast Asia at the time.

The Nanyang Style was a hybrid style, in that its proponents were all trained in both the Chinese ink painting and Western oil painting traditions; but they self-consciously chose to depict scenes in Southeast Asia — scenes that were neither Chinese nor Western.

Five major pioneer artists, four gentlemen and a lady, typify the Nanyang Style. All five of them had a common background, in that they were born in the treaty ports of China and, fleeing civil war in China, emigrated to Singapore in the 1940s. Hence, they painted from the point of view of an émigré attempting to reconcile one's self with a new home; and against the larger context of war and turbulence.

TOP: Life by the River. Liu Kang (1911–2004). 1975. Oil on canvas. 126 x 203 cm.

BOTTOM LEFT: Returning from Market. Cheong Soo Pieng (1917–1983). c. 1975. Oil on canvas. 117 x 96 cm.

BOTTOM RIGHT: Self-portrait. Georgette Chen (1906–1993). c. 1934. Oil on canvas. 35 x 27 cm.

The four gentlemen were Cheong Soo Pieng, Chen Chong Swee, Chen Wen Hsi and Liu Kang. They formed a tight-knit group, who found their artistic "voice", so to speak, from a trip they made together in 1952 to Bali. Having been inspired by the culture and the vibrant colours of Bali, they attempted to capture what they saw in a series of seminal works, each in their own style. This effort to incorporate Southeast Asian subjects into their traditional oil and ink painting traditions would later be considered the birth of Nanyang Style.

Of the four, Chen Wen Hsi was the oldest, having been born in 1906 in Canton province. He was as equally adept at oil painting as he was in Chinese ink painting. Of his entire body of work, he is most known for his series of gibbon paintings, delicately executed in traditional ink on paper. These paintings, depicting gibbons at play in the trees are full of life and vigour, demonstrating his love for nature and his attention to fine detail.

Chen Chong Swee was born in 1910 in the treaty port of Swatow. He painted in ink, watercolour and oil, blending a Chinese style of composition with Western watercolour techniques. He painted exclusively realist paintings; in particular, he loved to depict everyday scenes — local kampongs, fishing jetties, markets and bazaars, and women and men going about their daily life.

Liu Kang was born in 1911 in Engchun county, Hokkien province and worked primarily in oil. Trained in Paris and Shanghai, he was influenced by French Impressionist and Fauvist painters, specifically Matisse, van Gogh and Cezanne; and aspects of these artists' styles, in particular the use of bright, bold often unreal colours, would continue to be a defining feature of his work. All semblance to these earlier artists end there, however, and Liu Kang found his distinctive style in the depiction of everyday life in Singapore and Southeast Asia — kampongs, urban landscapes and scenes of people at work.

The youngest of the four was Cheong Soo Pieng, born in 1917 in Amoy. He painted in oil and watercolour, and he was known, in particular, for his distinctive, stylised depictions of Southeast Asian peoples very much inspired by traditional Balinese painting, into which he injected a sense of stateliness and timelessness. Of the four, he would venture most starkly outside of the realist realm, venturing into pure abstraction in the course of his career before returning to realism.

Finally, we come to the only lady artist of the group, Georgette Chen. Chen was born in Zhejiang province in 1906 to a very wealthy family. Her father had an antiques business in London, New York and Paris, so she spent her early years travelling between these cities, imbibing their art and culture. Trained in the Western tradition of oil painting in Paris, she was known for her still lifes, in particular still lifes that took tropical fruits and flowers as their subjects. She also excelled at portraits, and her most well-known work is perhaps the Self-Portrait she painted of herself in 1946, which depicted her being both detached and defiant at the same time.

Alcedo

CHAPTER FIVE

FLORA & FAUNA

SPICES AND THE SPICE TRADE

"The Malay merchants say God made Timor for sandalwood and Banda for mace and the Moluccas for cloves, and that this merchandise is not known anywhere else in the world except in these places."

— Tomé Pires, *The Suma Oriental* (1515)

Perhaps the single most important natural produce in history are those aromatic bits of nut, fruit, bud and bark we know as spices. A product of global trade since ancient times, the unquenchable demand for spices drove European powers eastwards and westwards in a frenzied bid to claim territories and thus establish a direct line of sight and supply to spice. It is no exaggeration to say that colonialism was the product of the Spice Trade, and that modern Singapore's existence is ultimately due to the demand for spices.

The word "spice" is derived from the French word *espice*, which in turn has as its root, the Latin term "species", referring to types of wares (rather than categories of animal and plant life). Throughout history, spices have been used for medicinal purposes, for enhancing the flavour of food, and for keeping food fresh. The variety of spices is dizzying, ranging from frankincense and myrrh from the Arab lands, to saffron from Persia, to ginger, cinnamon and pepper from India, to cloves, mace and nutmeg from Southeast Asia. Many of these were worth their weight in gold.

Up until the 1500s, the port city of Venice on the Adriatic Sea had an almost absolute monopoly on spices from the East, which reached the Most Serene Republic by ship and caravan from Constantinople and the Arab Lands beyond. For much of European history till the 1500s, spices were thus believed to have originated in exotic Arabia.

When the Ottomans took Constantinople in 1492 and thereafter cut off the supply of spices to Venice, the Europeans would take to the sea to secure a direct line of supply of these spices for themselves. It was then that they discovered the true origins of many of these spices — India and the islands of the East Indies. In particular, the origins of three specific spices — cloves, nutmeg and mace — were a mystery to the Europeans, and it wasn't until the 1500s that they discovered their source in the Moluccas, or fabled spice islands of the Malay Archipelago.

OPPOSITE: Black-capped Kingfisher. William Farquhar Collection of Natural History Drawings. Malacca, early 19th century.

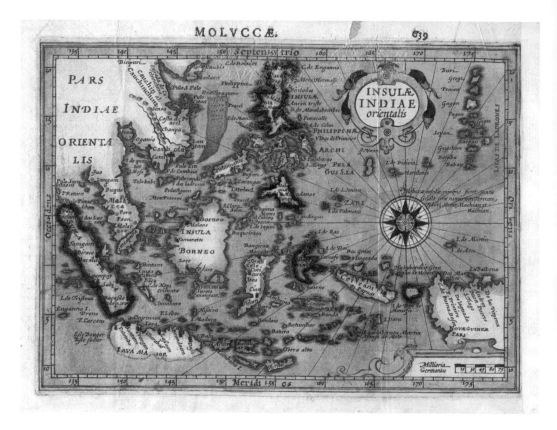

ABOVE: Map of Asia –
Insulae Indiae orientalis.
Gerhard Mercator.
c. 1607.

Of the many varieties of spices that are widely used today, about half a dozen of them formed the bulk of the Spice Trade. Black pepper, the dried fruit of the pepper tree (*Piper nigrum*), and cinnamon, the dried bark of the cinnamon tree (*Cinnamomum verum*), originate in the southern, tropical regions of India, and also Burma and Sri Lanka. They are perhaps the most familiar spices of all, with pepper being the single most traded spice in history, and certainly one spice that no contemporary cuisine can do without.

Cloves, nutmeg and mace are the three spices most closely associated with Southeast Asia — the early centuries of Portuguese and Dutch colonial efforts were undertaken in a bid to establish a worldwide monopoly in the trade of these spices. Cloves are the dried flower buds of the evergreen clove tree (*Syzygium aromaticum*). Brownish-red in colour, the buds have a very pungent, sweet scent, and they are often used to flavour curries and desserts. Cloves originate in the Molucca islands, and grow all over the archipelago.

Nutmeg and mace both derive from the same large, flowering tree (*Myristica fragrans*), with nutmeg being the seed of the fruit, and mace being the dried lattice that wraps around the seed. Nutmeg is indigenous to the

Banda islands, a remote chain of islands in eastern-most Indonesia. These islands may seem insignificant today, particularly since nutmeg has become far less important a crop than it was before, but one of the islands, Pulau Run, was famously ceded by the British to the Dutch in exchange for another then-deemed remote island in the New World: the island of Manhattan in what is today's New York City.

Other spices commonly used today include turmeric and ginger, both of which are rhizomes with a sharp, piercing flavour. Turmeric (*Curcuma domestica*), often used as a bright orange powder, originates in India and is a common ingredient in all kinds of curries and marinades for meat and poultry. Ginger (*Zingiber officinale*) is believed to have originated in southern China, and has a slightly more citrusy taste than its Indian cousin. Slivers and slices of ginger are used to flavour all manner of dishes in Chinese cuisine, while in Indian cuisine, ginger is also used as a fine, yellow powder.

Finally, another spice, unique to Southeast Asian and Chinese cuisine, is the star anise (*Illicium verum*), which is indigenous to southwestern China and northeast Vietnam. The fruit of the tree is used as the spice — these are eight-pointed star-shaped seed pods, which explains the name. Ground and powdered star anise is frequently combined with ginger, cinnamon, Sichuan peppers and cloves to make five-spice powder, which is in turn used in the preparation of many iconic Chinese dishes, like roast duck. Star anise is also a key component, alongside cinnamon, fennel, cardamom, cloves, coriander, pepper and nutmeg, in garam masala, which is used to flavour sauces and stews in Indian cuisine.

RIGHT: Nutmeg. William Farquhar Collection of Natural History Drawings. Malacca, early 19th century.

Singapore Botanic Gardens

"It abounds in an endless variety of plants equally interesting to the botanist, the agriculturist and the gardener, with unrivalled facilities and opportunities of disseminating these treasures and exchanging them for others."

— Letter from Nathaniel Wallich to Thomas
Stamford Raffles, November 1822

The idea for a Botanic Gardens in Singapore was first mooted by Raffles, almost immediately after he set up his residence on Government Hill. He got the idea in Java, where, during the British Interregnum between 1811 and 1815, he ruled the island as its Lieutenant-Governor.

While Governor, he resided, like all the Dutch governors before him, at the Governor's Mansion in Buitenzorg (today's Bogor), situated some 60 kilometres south of the capital Batavia and on higher ground with a much cooler climate. He lived in an old VOC mansion and had the gardens re-landscaped into an English style botanical gardens. His first wife, Olivia Marianne Raffles, had died during his tenure in Java, and a memorial to her had been erected in these gardens. The gardens were officially designated the National Botanical Gardens in 1817. Meanwhile, Raffles was sent onwards to Bencoolen and thereafter to Singapore, where our story began.

BELOW: Entrance gates to Singapore Botanic Gardens, early 20th century.

In 1822, a close friend of Raffles, Danish surgeon and naturalist, Nathaniel Wallich, came to visit in Singapore. Wallich, a former employee of the Danish East India Company, had also just been appointed Super-

ABOVE: Palm valley, Singapore Botanic Gardens, early 20th century.

intendent of the Calcutta Botanical Gardens in 1817, a post he would hold until 1846. While in Singapore, Wallich and Raffles spent many hours together, discussing the merits of establishing a Botanical Gardens — similar to those in Calcutta and Buitenzorg — in Singapore. The former was convinced enough to write a highly persuasive proposal to the Colonial Government in Calcutta. The proposal was viewed favourably, and funding was dispatched to Singapore for the purposes of constructing a 19-hectare "Botanical and Experimental Gardens" on Government Hill.

These gardens were the forerunner to today's Singapore Botanic Gardens. They didn't last long, having been shut down and sold off by 1829. In 1859, a new Botanic Gardens were established at Tanglin, on the edge of the verdant, plantation-lined Orchard Road. The instigators of the project were an agri-horticultural society, though the Gardens were later handed over to the British colonial government for maintenance.

As originally established, the Singapore Botanic Gardens sat on 23 hectares of undeveloped land, including a 6-hectare parcel of primary forest (which still exists in the Gardens today). Many of the Gardens' distinguishing features, introduced by its first superintendent, Laurence Niven, still exist today. These include Bandstand Hill, Swan Lake and the superintendent's residence, known today as Burkill Hall after a later superintendent.

Even though their initial function was purely recreational, by the 1870s the Gardens had become a centre for scientific research. Many of the early Superintendents of the Gardens had been trained at the Royal Botanic Gardens at Kew, England. Of these, the most notorious of them is perhaps naturalist Henry Nicholas Ridley, who, in 1877, brought rubber seedlings from Kew to Singapore, and successfully experimenting with their propagation, eventually introduced seedlings for cultivation throughout the Malayan Peninsula. Ridley's work would result in the establishment of rubber as a major cash crop in Malaya then and today.

The Gardens continued to expand in the course of the 1900s under successive superintendents. The 1930s saw significant milestones in the Gardens' history, including the establishment of its famous orchid breeding and hybridisation programme, still vital today; and the iconic white Bandstand on Bandstand Hill.

Today, the Botanic Gardens occupy an area of about 74 hectares and continue to play a vital role in the city-state's cultural life. They are popular with Singaporeans and foreign residents alike, and are one of the most important centres for botanical research in the world. The Gardens boast a "collection" of some 36,400 living plants from 6,544 species; while its herbarium contains some 750,000 specimens.

On 4th July 2015, in recognition of the Gardens' historical and cultural significance, they were inscribed by UNESCO as a World Heritage Site — Singapore's first.

The William Farquhar Collection of Natural History Drawings

The William Farquhar Collection of Natural History Drawings consists of 477 watercolours of flora and fauna, indigenous to Malacca, Singapore and the Malayan Peninsula. It was commissioned by Major William Farquhar between 1819 and 1823, when he was First Resident of Singapore. Farquhar had earlier resided in Malacca and he had been impressed with the variety and diversity of wildlife in the Malayan rainforest.

The drawings were designed to be scientifically accurate, and many of them are so detailed as to be lifelike. The name of the artist — or artists — is lost to us, but it is generally accepted that he (or they) were Chinese artists of the Canton school of export painting. Each of the drawings has the scientific name of the plant or animal in question inscribed, alongside the common name in Jawi Malay and English. They are thus interesting pieces of cross-cultural art, having been commissioned by a European, drawn by Chinese, and featuring Malayan wildlife.

In style, the drawings come from an earlier-established tradition of Indian Company School Natural History paintings. These were extremely accurate, scientific paintings of Indian flora and fauna, commissioned by a generation of English sahibs and memsahibs of local Indian water-colourists. One need only recall the immense collections of the Marquis of Wellesley (1760–1842), Governor-General of Calcutta (more than 2,500 drawings); or that of Lord Clive (1754–1839) when he was Governor of Madras (more than 1,500 drawings). Company School natural history drawings were popular from the late 1700s all through to the mid 1800s, when the advent of photography rendered such paintings obsolete.

Perhaps the most exquisite of these collections of Company School Natural History Drawings, and, indeed, a worthy predecessor to the William Farquhar Collection, was the Lady Impey Collection, or the Impey Album. Lady Mary Impey (1749–1818), wife of Elijah Impey, Chief Justice of Fort William, Calcutta, had, in the course of the late 1770s to mid 1780s, commissioned a series of more than 300 watercolours of local birds and animals. Of these, many were undersigned by one Shaikh Zayn al-Din, a Muslim Bengali painter. Unfortunately, the Impey Album has not survived in its entirety, with many pieces scattered around the world in private and institutional hands.

Another significant collection that was a contemporary of the Farquhar Collection was the Raffles Collection — a selection of natural history drawings that Stamford Raffles had commissioned during his time in the Malayan Peninsula. Unfortunately, the bulk of these drawings perished en route back to London, leaving only a single volume of 129 watercolours of birds from Sumatra in the Library of the India Office.

Rhinoceros Hornbill (top) and Slow Loris (bottom). William Farquhar Collection of Natural History Drawings, Malacca, early 19th century.

In a stroke of fate, the William Farquhar Collection has been handed down in its entirety. Farquhar had donated these drawings to the Royal Asiatic Society of Great Britain and Ireland in 1826, where they remained, more or less, until 1993, when the Society put them up for auction by Sotheby's in London. A Singaporean benefactor, Goh Geok Khim, acquired the Collection and generously donated it to the National Museum of Singapore, where it continues to reside today.

The Collection includes 251 drawings of plants, 108 of birds, 60 of mammals, reptiles and invertebrates, and 58 of fish. One of the most memorable of these drawings is that of a Black-capped Kingfisher (*Halcyon pileata*), captured with its wings fully spread, about to land (or take off) from the branch it sits on. The black-capped kingfisher is a common bird in Singapore, often first observed as a quick flash of blue diving into Singapore's lakes and canals in a bid to snatch a meal from the water.

Another magnificent drawing is that of the Rhinoceros Hornbill (*Buceros rhinoceros*), one of the largest birds in the Malayan Peninsula, and one that can be seen occasionally in the jungles of Singapore's various nature reserves and even in the verdant, tree-lined roads and sidewalks in Bukit Timah, in the vicinity of Bukit Timah Nature Reserve.

A highlight in the mammalian section is the drawing of the Malayan Tapir (*Acrocodia indica*) with its black and white pelt and its distinctive curled snout. Farquhar also had commissioned a drawing of a juvenile tapir with its white on black mottled pelt. Farquhar had been the first Briton to describe the Malayan Tapir, though Raffles later tried to discredit Farquhar and have the "discovery" of the tapir attributed to him.

Another very popular drawing is that of the Slow Loris (*Nycticebus coucang*), staring straight at the viewer with its orange-gold eyes, and holding on to a branch with its four legs. Both loris and tapir are indigenous to the Malay Peninsula, but are very rare in Singapore.

Finally, perhaps the most delightful of all these drawings is the one commissioned of ornamental goldfish (*Carassius auratus*). The scene is idyllic: six goldfish frolic and flap their fins in what must have been a pond. Their tails are spread wide to best display their vibrant colours. The plate shows that even in Farquhar's time, in the early 1800s, the breeding and rearing of goldfish was already commonplace. More importantly, the dynamic, colourful composition of the painting demonstrates that these natural history drawings were more than just scientific documents; they were works of art in their own right.

SANG KANCIL, OR THE CLEVER MOUSE-DEER

The Lesser Mouse-deer (*Tragulus kanchil*) is the smallest species of deer in the world. It is indigenous to the jungles of Southeast Asia, in particular, those of Malaysia, Indonesia and Singapore. In Malay, the Lesser Mousedeer is known as *kancil*, and it features as the lead character in an entire tradition of Malay folktales.

The Sang Kancil Tales — *Sang* being a term of respect, sort of like "Mister" — are part of a larger oral tradition of children's folk tales and legends in the Malay world. Sang Kancil is equivalent to Brer Rabbit in the Western tradition. He is a clever underdog who consistently outwits far larger enemies in the jungle; those who would devour him for lunch.

A popular tale has the mouse-deer wishing to cross the river to get to fruit trees on the other side. However, the river is infested with *buaya*, or crocodiles, all desirous of having him for a meal. Crocodiles are the largest natural aquatic predator in Singapore and the Malay World. The local species is the Estuarine Crocodile (*Crocodylus porosus*), also known as the salt-water crocodile. This species is known to inhabit brackish local rivers in the Malayan Peninsula, and such crocodiles have been known to occasionally surface in Singapore's man-made reservoirs. The Estuarine Crocodile can grow to almost eight metres in length and thus, may easily consume a Lesser Mouse-deer in a single, decisive chomp.

Sang Kancil, knowing full well the voracious nature of buaya, calls out to one of them, announcing that the Sultan of the Kampong was having a feast to which everyone, including the crocodiles, was to be invited. But first, the crocodiles would have to suffer themselves be counted by the mouse-deer, in order that the Sultan may know how many places to set for his guests.

The crocodiles, flushed with pride and taken in by Sang Kancil's tall tale, begin to line themselves up in a row, offering the wily mouse deer a natural

RIGHT: Mouse-deer relief at Candi Prambanan, Central Java, Indonesia.

bridge to the other side of the river. As he hops gingerly from one crocodile's head to the next, Sang Kancil counts "One, two, three, four" and so on, until he reaches the other side of the river, whereupon he turns back to laugh at the crocodiles and thank them for having helped him cross the river.

Another popular tale has Sang Kancil take on the tiger, or *harimau*. The local species in Singapore and the Malayan Peninsula is the Malayan Tiger (*Panthera tigris jacksoni*), a subspecies of tiger closely related to the Sumatran Tiger. Up until the early 1900s, tigers once roamed wild in the interior of Singapore, particularly around Bukit Timah, where they would occasionally emerge from the jungle to take livestock and poultry. Tiger hunting became a sport for much of the mid-1800s to early 1900s, with the last wild tiger in Singapore only killed in the 1930s, while it was roaming around the Choa Chu Kang area.

The tiger holds a pre-eminent place in Malay and Singaporean myth and folklore, being the paramount predator in these parts. The tiger was a primordial force, a symbol of the ravenous powers of the jungle, as opposed to the structured orderliness of the kampong. Tiger spirits, or *hantu belian*, are powerful spirits that can be either malevolent or benevolent. They are known to haunt sacred places (*keramat*) — ruins, shrines and old wells, often deep in the jungle, far away from human civilization. The most powerful *bomohs*, or Malay shamans, were also known as *bomoh belian*, as they were believed to contain within them, tiger spirits, that in the light of the full moon, would cause them to morph into fearsome were-tigers, or *harimau jadi-jadian*.

Our protagonist, Sang Kancil, is set upon one day by just such a fearsome tiger. As he sips water at the edge of the riverbank, Sang Harimau emerges from the jungle and looms over our tiny hero. He declares, in his booming baritone, that he would devour Kancil that very instant, and that the mouse-deer had better cower in fright, if he knew what was good for him.

Clever Kancil, the wheels turning swiftly in his head, turns around and begins to praise and flatter the tiger incessantly, calling him the mightiest and most powerful Sultan in the jungle — save one. This powerful Sultan was none other, so Kancil explains, than the mouse deer's patron liege, the Sultan of his kampong, who was far larger than Tiger, and would most likely defeat Tiger in any fight.

Tiger is dismayed and compels the mouse-deer to take him to this mighty Sultan. Whereupon Kancil takes the tiger through a winding circuitous route through the jungle back to exactly the same spot on the river bank. Pointing to Tiger's reflection in the water, he declares it his Liege. Failing to recognise his own reflection, the tiger jumps into the water, and is promptly swept away by the current. Meanwhile, the clever mouse-deer makes his well-deserved escape.

THE BOY AND THE SWORDFISH

A popular legend that pertains to Singapore specifically is that of the Swordfish attack on Singapore, and the humble young boy who saved the day. The legend, contained in the *Sejarah Melayu*, or *The Malay Annals*, recounts the tale.

In the early of days of the Kingdom of Singapura, the island kingdom was plagued by swordfish. It was recounted that waves of these malevolent swordfish leapt from the shore without notice, stabbed victims in their chest and waist, relieved them of their heads, and generally made a massacre of the orang laut that happened to inhabit the seashore.

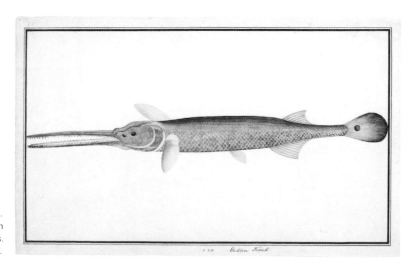

RIGHT: Garfish (ikan todak). William Farquhar Collection of Natural History Drawings. Malacca, early 19th century.

ABOVE: Singapore, New Harbour, early 20th century.

This plague of swordfish continued for months and occurred suddenly. Large numbers of the orang laut perished by swordfish, so much so that whenever an attack was imminent, an alarm would be sounded in the *kampong air*, or water village. The Raja himself, alarmed by the huge number of casualties, came down to the seashore to examine the carnage.

Determined to protect his people, the Raja ordered his guards to form a human wall along the seashore. But when the swordfish came, they fell like rain, killing and injuring these brave men who had sacrificed themselves for the protection of their people.

This was when a voice rang out from amongst the gathered village folk; the voice of a young lad, who cried out, "Why are we sacrificing our men folk by using them as barricades? Why not make a barricade of banana stems instead? That way, when the swordfish attack, their swords would be caught in the stems, and we may cut them down."

The Raja and his people, realising the boy was right, did exactly as he suggested. The next time the swordfish attacked, they found themselves stuck to the banana stems, whereupon they were killed and cut down in huge numbers. As wave after wave descended upon the shore, so did the large fish find themselves caught upon the stems and slayed by the villagers. Finally, there were no more.

In the aftermath of this success, the Raja called for a celebration in all Singapura, and heralded the brilliance and bravery of the young boy. Unfortunately, he fell prey to the words of an ill-judged advisor, who advised him to be rid of the boy, for fear the latter would grow up to be a very wise man who would threaten the Raja's sovereignty.

Thus, the Raja gave orders for the boy to be executed. But when the boy was executed, his blood flowed for weeks until it stained the very soil itself red. The place where he is supposed to have been executed was named Bukit Merah, or Red Hill, and it exists to this very day.

In the meantime, it must be noted that there are no swordfish indigenous to the waters of the Singapore Straits, nor are swordfish known to venture in the shallows. Instead, one finds varieties of needlefish or garfish (*Tylosurus crocodilus*), known generically in Malay as *ikan todak*. These are endowed with a swordlike beak and are known to leap from the shallows at high speeds. At these speeds, their beaks are capable of puncturing human skin, and causing great injury to the victim. These perhaps, are the swordfish of the legend, and indeed, resemble the latter in all outward form.

VANDA MISS JOAQUIM — SINGAPORE'S NATIONAL FLOWER

"A few years ago Miss Joaquim, a lady residing in Singapore, well-known for her success as a horticulturist, succeeded in crossing Vanda hookeriana, Rchb. f., and Vanda teres, two plants cultivated in almost every garden in Singapore..."

— Sir Henry Ridley, *The Gardener's Chronicle*, 24th June 1893

The Vanda Miss Joaquim's story mirrors that of Singapore, in that it is a cross-cultural East-West and East-East hybrid of an orchid. It was the result of a crossing between the *Vanda hookeriana*, an orchid indigenous to Malaya, and the *Vanda teres*, an orchid from Burma. The instigator of this crossing was an Armenian lady, Miss Agnes Joaquim (1854–1899).

The late Agnes Joaquim was an accomplished horticulturist, known for her "green thumb", so to speak. Between 1881 and 1899, she won a whopping 70-odd awards and recognitions in Singapore for the breeding and cultivation of various kinds of fruit, vegetables and flowers. She had inherited this knack for botany and gardening from her family, upstanding members of the tiny Armenian community in Singapore. Notably, her father, Parsick Joaquim, had served on the Board of the Botanical Gardens while her brother, Joe Joaquim had also served on a committee of the Gardens.

While there has been some controversy historically as to the exact origins of the orchid — namely questions as to whether Agnes had actually created the hybrid, or merely discovered the hybrid growing naturally in her garden — official recognition has been given (only just) to Agnes as the breeder of her namesake orchid.

BELOW: Portrait of Ms Agnes Joaquim.

Agnes first presented the orchid in 1893 to the then-Superintendent of the Botanic Gardens, Sir Henry Ridley, making it the earliest recorded orchid hybrid in Singapore. Ridley subsequently "debuted" the orchid in *The Gardeners' Chronicle*, a horticulturalists' periodical in London in June that same year, noting its hybrid nature and attributing its creation to Miss Agnes Joaquim.

Subsequently, the Vanda Miss Joaquim, as it came to be known, was also brought on a roadshow where it was displayed at the Royal Horticultural Show in London in 1897 and at a Flower Show in Singapore in 1899, where it also won first prize for its rarity and beauty.

And indeed, the orchid is a beautiful work of art. In form, the blossom is shapely and well proportioned, with hints of curls in its sepals, suggesting a genteel frailty in its overall composition. Its sepals gradate from white to a pale lilac-pink, with its lip a deep fuchsia, and its heart a burning yellow-gold.

The Vanda Miss Joaquim occurs in dense clumps of flowering stands at the top of the orchid plant itself, which grows tall and requires artificial support. The plant only flowers when it has reached 40 to 50 centimetres in height, making this Vanda one of the largest orchid plants in the world. At the Singapore Botanic Gardens, a few groves of it may be found in the National Orchid Gardens and elsewhere, flowering profusely and exploding in a riot of pink and white.

Unfortunately, Agnes Joaquim died in 1899 of cancer, at the age of 45. Her legacy lives on in the Vanda Miss Joaquim, designated Singapore's National Flower in 1981.

DURIAN, KING OF FRUITS

"The Durian grows on a large and lofty forest-tree, something resembling an Elm in character, but with a more smooth and scaly bark. The fruit is round or slightly oval, about the size of a small melon, of a green colour, and covered with strong spines, the bases of which touch each other, and are consequently somewhat hexagonal, while the points are very strong and sharp. [...] The five cells are silky-white within, and are filled with a mass of firm, cream-coloured pulp, containing about three seeds each. This pulp is the eatable part, and its consistence and flavour are indescribable. A rich custard highly flavoured with almonds gives the best general idea of it, but there are occasional wafts of flavour that call to mind cream-cheese, onion-sauce, sherry-wine, and other incongruous dishes. Then there is a rich glutinous smoothness in the pulp which nothing else possesses, but which adds to its delicacy. It is neither acid nor sweet nor juicy; yet it wants neither of these qualities, for it is in itself perfect. It produces no nausea or other bad effect, and the more you eat of it the less you feel inclined to stop. In fact, to eat Durians is a new sensation worth a voyage to the East to experience."

— Alfred Russell Wallace, *The Malay Archipelago* (1856)

The durian (*Durio zibethinus*) is endemic to the Malay Archipelago, and is one of the most notorious of the region's many endemic varieties of fruit. The word "durian" derives from the Malay word *duri* or thorny, so the name of the fruit literally just means "that which is thorny".

RIGHT: Durian. William Farquhar Collection of Natural History Drawings. Malacca, early 19th century.

As its name suggests, the durian is distinguished by its exterior, which resembles a sort of thorny, green mace (the mediaeval weapon, not the tropical spice). But crack open the thorny shell, and the inside of the fruit reveals succulent flesh that surrounds large, egg-like seeds. This pungent flesh, sometimes silky white and other times yellow-gold, affords the durian its notoriety. For those unaccustomed to it, durian smells and tastes alternately like vomit or sewage. For those who swear by durian, its odour is the most delicious scent in the world. That notwithstanding, the durian is perhaps the only fruit banned all over the world in airline cabins, hotels and other forms of public transport, due to its pungent aroma.

Most Southeast Asians are accustomed to eating durian, and regard it as the king of all fruits. Certainly, in Singapore, durians are consumed avidly, particularly during "durian season", which occurs between the months of June and August each year. The most favoured varieties are those with yellow-gold flesh that melts in the mouth and tastes — as Alfred Russell Wallace recalls — like custard with almonds and sherry thrown into the mix. The ritual of consuming durian is often a communal one, with family and friends gathering to watch as the fruit is opened with a heavy knife and a strong hand, and then partaking eagerly as the large fleshy seeds are distributed around the mat.

The durian grows on a large tree which reaches up to 50 metres in height. Most varieties of durian that are eaten today are cultivated, though certainly the wild varieties continue to grow and survive in the jungles of Southeast Asia. The large, fragrant durian blossoms flower in the afternoon, and are pollinated by large nocturnal fruit bats. Durian trees can also be dangerous, as the fruit grows copiously from any branch of the tree, and upon ripening, falls from the branch; any unsuspecting passers-by hit by the fruit could be killed immediately.

Besides eating the durian raw, the flesh of the durian is also used in Singapore, Malaysia and Thailand to make a variety of traditional sweets and desserts, most notably durian cakes which are unlike any other cake. Taking the form of baton-shaped cylinders, they are made from a paste-like candy that is a mix of durian flesh and sugar. More recently in Singapore, durian flesh has found itself in more contemporary desserts such as durian sponge cakes, durian custard puffs and durian ice cream, in a testament to the enduring popularity of this King of Fruits.

ABOVE: Visiting Bukit
Timah Nature Reserve,
Singapore, 1894.

THE LURE OF THE JUNGLE

The jungle, or tropical rainforest, is the natural state of things in Singapore and much of the Malay Archipelago, city-state and island chain sit squarely in the equatorial belt. In both Malay and European tradition, the jungle has come to signify a dark, overgrown, primordial realm; the exact counterpoint to civilisation, or the realm of man.

In Malay folklore, the jungle is a dangerous place: the preserve of not only wild animals, but other wild things like spirits (*hantu*), vampires (*pontianak*) and even more fearsome creatures like the were-tiger (harimau jadi-jadian). It is known as the *alam liar*, or "the wild place"; and when one meets someone in the wild place, one should always think twice before taking him or her back to one's dwelling place.

In Western tradition, particularly due to influence from the British Raj, the jungle represents pagan unruliness, as opposed to European orderliness. The jungle is a dark, forbidding force, but one that may be controlled and overcome; cleared away and replaced with orderly townships and cities. That said, in Rudyard Kipling's *The Jungle Book*, prevailing colonial notions of the jungle as lawless wild lands are turned over on their head, as Kipling repeatedly evokes "the law of the jungle".

There are two kinds of jungle/rainforest. Primary rainforest refers to tracts of jungle that have never been cleared by man. These are often thickly overgrown, with canopies that may blot out the light of the sun. Primary rainforests are cradles of biodiversity, with one square mile of rainforest holding more plant and animal species than the whole of North America.

Secondary rainforest refers to re-grown jungle — jungle that has grown on land previously cleared by man. These forests are a little sparser in terms of tree and plant cover, but when left alone long enough, can grow to be as thickly forested as primary rainforest.

As Singapore is a highly urbanised place, most of its rainforest has been cleared for roads and townships. The only exception is in the centre of the island around Bukit Timah ("Tin Hill"), the tallest hill on the island. This area has been designated a Central Water Catchment Area and Nature Reserve: the Bukit Timah Nature Reserve.

The Reserve was first created in 1884 upon the recommendation of the Superintendent of the Botanic Gardens, who also suggested the creation of a Forestry Department to manage the Reserve. Some 30 years earlier in 1854, Alfred Russell Wallace — famed for having articulated the Wallace Line and independently describing the process of evolution — had spent a few months in the vicinity of Bukit Timah, and remarked on the diversity of flora and fauna on the hill slopes of Bukit Timah.

However, commercial imperatives had caused for much of the tree cover around Bukit Timah to be cut down in the late 1800s and replaced with

ABOVE: Bukit Timah
Nature Reserve, c. 1845.

stands of commercial hardwoods and other cash crops such as rubber trees. Between 1884 and the turn of the 19th century, much of the land in the Reserve, having earlier been cleared, was left to re-forest, resulting in the Bukit Timah Nature Reserve as we know it today.

The Reserve today is 163 hectares in size. It supports more than 1,000 species of plants and more than 500 species of animals. Amongst these are critically endangered animals such as the Sunda pangolin (*Manis javanica*) and the Banded Leaf Monkey (*Presbytis femoralis*). It is also home to more well-known species such as the Lesser Mouse-deer, the Rhinoceros Hornbill, and up until the early 1900s, the Malayan Tiger.

Aside from the small grove of virgin rainforest in the Botanic Gardens, the largest tract of primary rainforest in Singapore occurs here in Bukit Timah Nature Reserve, where 40 percent of the rainforest is primary. The forest is home to a magnificent array of ancient forest giants, including stands of Shorea, Tembusu and Dipterocarps. It is a much-needed urban green lung amidst one of the most dynamic, heavily populated and fastest growing urban centres in the world.

RIGHT: Travellers' palm, early 20th century.

THE TRAVELLERS' PALM

The Travellers' Palm (*Ravenala madagascariensis*) features in the landscape of Old Singapore, particularly in the private, landscaped gardens of hotels, colonial black-and-whites and private residences, as well as in wayside greenery. In fact, it features rather prominently in the minds of travellers to the region as being a key feature of the Southeast Asian landscape.

Ironically, the Travellers' Palm is not native to Singapore or Southeast Asia at all, but hails originally from the African island of Madagascar, and was brought here by the British in the early 1900s. In addition, the palm isn't even a true palm but is closely related to the banana tree, as well as those strange, colourful ornamental plants known as Heliconias. It is so called, because one supposedly is able to slake one's thirst by drinking the water that collects between the sheaths of its leaves. But that is an urban legend, since this water is often murky and putrid and should never be drunk.

The Travellers' Palm is easily recognisable for its large oar-shaped leaves which grow outwards in a distinctive fan shape. The tree is hardy and grows anywhere in the tropics and subtropics where there is bright sunlight. The "fan" of the tree tends to grow along an east-west axis, such that the "face" of the fan is oriented north-south.

In Singapore, the most obvious place to find the Travellers' Palm is in the gardens of Raffles Hotel. The Raffles Hotels and Resorts group also features the Traveller's Palm prominently as its corporate logo.

OTTERS IN THE CITY

Smooth-coated otters (*Lutrogale perspicillata*) are indigenous to Southern India and Southeast Asia. Social creatures, they typically live and hunt in family groups including parents and young. They live on fish primarily, but also other crustaceans and shellfish. In Singapore, they are categorised as "Critically Endangered" and sightings used to be exceptionally rare. The first sighting was in 1936 on Lazarus Island, and the second in 1990 in the Sungei Buloh Nature Reserve.

All that changed from 2015, when families of these otters started appearing in urban parks and water bodies all over Singapore. The first group was spotted in Bishan-Ang Mo Kio Park, a park created from greening and re-landscaping what once used to be a large drainage and rainwater canal. Then another family started appearing in Sentosa, where its members preyed on expensive ornamental koi in the ponds of wealthy bankers' residences at Sentosa Cove. Finally, a family appeared in the waters of Marina Bay, just off the brand-new Gardens by the Bay. This family can be seen from time to time swimming up the Singapore River to feast on fish

RIGHT: Otters playing in Marina Bay, against Singapore's contemporary skyline.

and to sunbathe alongside the Asian Civilisations Museum and the towering skyscrapers of Raffles Place.

Their re-appearance in the city is testament to decades of work the Singaporean Government — in particular, the departments managing the city-state's parks and water bodies — has done in cleaning up its rivers and other water bodies, and in greening the city in general. The Singapore River, festering and polluted for much of its history, was extensively cleaned up in the 1980s, and today, apparently holds enough fish for a family of otters to survive on. Elsewhere, the Government's decision to make reservoirs of the former Kallang River and Marina Bay has effectively turned these into bodies of freshwater, capable of supporting entire riverine ecosystems.

The return of indigenous wildlife to what is perhaps the most urbanised and densely populated place on earth, and the co-existence between wild and urban distinguishes, and will continue to distinguish, Singapore from other cosmopolitan urban centres in the region and the world. In the meantime, the otters are here to stay, and they are watched over by legions of local fans, who have taken them in as honorary Singaporeans and who take pride in how Singapore has lived up to its Garden City status; nay, surpassed it to be a Rainforest City.

Bibliography

Introduction and General

Borschberg, Peter (Ed.), 2017. *Admiral Matelieff's Singapore and Johor, 1606 – 1616*. Singapore: NUS Press.

Cheah, Jin Seng, 2007. *Singapore – 500 Early Postcards*. Singapore: Editions Didier Millet.

Dorai, Francis and Chee, Veronica (Eds.), 2017. *The Rare Materials Collection – Selections from the National Library Singapore*. Singapore: National Library Board.

Frost, Mark R. & Balasingham-Chow, Yu-Mei, 2013. *Singapore – A Biography*. Singapore: Editions Didier Millet.

Gipouloux, François, 2009. *La Méditerranée asiatique – villes portuaires et réseaux marchands en Chine, Japon et en Asie du Sud-Est, XVIe – XXIe siècle*. Paris: CNF Editions.

Jayapal, M., 1992. *Old Singapore*. Singapore: Oxford University Press.

Koh, Tommy et al (Eds.), 2006. *Singapore – The Encyclopedia*. Singapore: Editions Didier Millet in association with the National Heritage Board.

Kong, Lily, 2011. *Conserving the past, creating the future: Urban heritage in Singapore*. Singapore: Urban Redevelopment Authority.

Kwa, Chong Guan, 2017. *Singapore Chronicles: PRE-COLONIAL SINGAPORE*. Singapore: Institute of Policy Studies and Straits Times Press.

Kwa, Chong Guan, Heng, Derek and Tan, Tai Yong, 2009. *Singapore: A 700-Year History*. Singapore: National Archives of Singapore.

Kwok, Kian Woon et al, 1999. *Our Place in Time: Exploring Heritage and Memory in Singapore*. Singapore: Singapore Heritage Society.

Lai, Chee Kien, 2015. *Through the Lens of Lee Kip Lin: Photographs of Singapore 1965 – 1995*. Singapore: Editions Didier Millet.

Liu, Gretchen, 1999. *Singapore: A Pictorial History 1819 – 2000*. Singapore: Archipelago Press and National Heritage Board.

Miksic, John N., 2013. *Singapore & the Silk Road of the Sea, 1300-1800*. Singapore: NUS Press.

National Heritage Board, 2002. *Singapore's 100 Historic Places*. Singapore: Archipelago Press.

Savage, Victor R. and Yeoh, Brenda S. A., 2003. *Toponymics - A Study of Singapore Street Names*. Singapore: Eastern Universities Press.

Tarling, Nicholas, 2015. *Singapore Chronicles: COLONIAL SINGAPORE*. Singapore: Institute of Policy Studies and Straits Times Press.

Ting, Kennie, 2015. *The Romance of the Grand Tour – 100 Years of Travel in South East Asia*. Singapore: Talisman Publishing.

Ting, Kennie, 2015. *Singapore Chronicles: HERITAGE*. Singapore: Institute of Policy Studies and Straits Times Press.

Tun Sri Lanang, 1612. *Sejarah Melayu (The Malay Annals)*. Translated by Dr. John Leyden, 1821. Kuala Lumpur: Silverfish Malaysian Classics.

Turnbull, Constance Mary, 2009. *A History of Modern Singapore, 1819-2005*. Singapore: NUS Press.

Wan, Meng Hao, & Lau, Jacqueline, 2009. *Heritage Places of Singapore*. Singapore: Marshall Cavendish Editions.

Wong, Hong Suen, 2010. *Singapore through 19th Century Prints & Paintings*. Singapore: Editions Didier Millet and National Museum of Singapore.

People & Places

Abdullah Abdul Kadir, 1949. *The Hikayat Abdullah: The autobiography of Abdullah bin Abdul Kadir, 1797–1854*. Translated from the Malay by the Rev. E. G. Shellabear. Singapore: Methodist Publishing House.

Auger, Timothy, 2015. *A River Transformed: Singapore River and Marina Bay*. Singapore: Editions Didier Millet.

Barley, Nigel, 2010. *In the Footsteps of Stamford Raffles*. Singapore: Monsoon Books Pte. Ltd.

Bastin, John S., 2009. *Letters and books of Sir Stamford Raffles and Lady Raffles: The Tang Holdings Collection of autograph letters and books of Sir Stamford Raffles and Lady Raffles*. Singapore: Editions Didier Millet.

Bastin, John S., 2014. *Raffles and Hastings: Private Exchanges behind the Founding of Singapore*. Singapore: National Library Board.

Bastin, John S. and Weizenegger, Julie, 2016. *The family of Sir Stamford Raffles*. Singapore: Editions Didier Millet.

Boulger, Demetrius Charles, 1897. *The Life of Sir Stamford Raffles*. London: Horace Marshall & Son.

Buckley, Charles Burton, 1902. *An Anecdotal History of Old Times in Singapore, 1819–1867*. Singapore: Fraser and Neave, Limited.

Chua, Alvin, 2016. "Fort Canning Cemetery". *Singapore Infopedia*. Singapore: National Library Board. Available at: http://eresources.nlb.gov.sg/infopedia/articles/SIP_1685_2010-07-14.html?s=fort%20canning%20cemetery

Cornelius, Vernon, 1999. "Collyer Quay." *Singapore Infopedia*. Singapore: National Library Board. Available at: http://eresources.nlb.gov.sg/infopedia/articles/SIP_218_2005-01-19.html?s=-fullerton.

Cornelius, Vernon, 2016. "Cavenagh Bridge." *Singapore Infopedia*. Singapore: National Library Board. Available at: http://eresources.nlb.gov.sg/infopedia/articles/SIP_2_2004-12-17.html?s=-cavenagh%20bridge.

Cornelius, Vernon, 2016. "Coleman Bridge." *Singapore Infopedia*. Singapore: National Library Board. Available at: http://eresources.nlb.gov.sg/infopedia/

articles/SIP_151_2004-12-16.html?s=-coleman%20bridge.

Cornelius, Vernon, 2016. "Collyer Quay." *Singapore Infopedia*. Singapore: National Library Board. Available at: http://eresources.nlb.gov.sg/infopedia/articles/SIP_218_2005-01-19.html?s=collyer%20quay.

Cornelius, Vernon, 2016. "G.D. Coleman". *Singapore Infopedia*. Singapore: National Library Board. Available at: http://eresources.nlb.gov.sg/infopedia/articles/SIP_134_2004-12-10.html?s=GD%20Coleman.

Cornelius, Vernon, 2016. "Read Bridge." *Singapore Infopedia*. Singapore: National Library Board. Available at: http://eresources.nlb.gov.sg/infopedia/articles/SIP_28_2004-12-24.html?s=ord%20bridge.

Cornelius, Vernon and Loo, Janice, 2016. "Anderson Bridge." *Singapore Infopedia*. Singapore: National Library Board. Available at: http://eresources.nlb.gov.sg/infopedia/articles/SIP_923_2004-12-24.html?s=anderson%20bridge.

Cornelius-Takahama, Vernon, 2001. "Boat Quay." *Singapore Infopedia*. Singapore: National Library Board. Available at: http://eresources.nlb.gov.sg/infopedia/articles/SIP_224_2004-12-20.html?s=boat%20quay.

Cornelius-Takahama, Vernon, 2016. "Elgin Bridge." *Singapore Infopedia*. Singapore: National Library Board. Available at: http://eresources.nlb.gov.sg/infopedia/articles/SIP_921_2004-12-10.html?s=clemenceau%20bridge.

Cornelius-Takahama, Vernon, 2016. "Fort Canning Park". *Singapore Infopedia*. Singapore: National Library Board. Available at: http://eresources.nlb.gov.sg/infopedia/articles/SIP_8_2004-12-10.html.

Cornelius-Takahama, Vernon, 2016. "Singapore River Communities" *Singapore Infopedia*. Singapore: National Library Board. Available at: http://eresources.nlb.gov.sg/infopedia/arti-

cles/SIP_498_2004-12-27.html?s=singapore%20river.

Cornelius-Takahama, Vernon, 2016. "Singapore Stone." *Singapore Infopedia*. Singapore: National Library Board. Available at: http://eresources.nlb.gov.sg/infopedia/articles/SIP_43_2005-01-26.html?s=singapore%20stone.

Cornelius-Takahama, Vernon and Wang, Damien, 2016. "Singapore River (historical overview)" *Singapore Infopedia*. Singapore: National Library Board. Available at: http://eresources.nlb.gov.sg/infopedia/articles/SIP_148_2005-02-02.html?s=singapore%20river.

Coupland, Reginald, 1946. *Raffles of Singapore*. Third Edition. UK: Collins.

Crawfurd, John, 1830. *Journal of an Embassy from the Governor-General of India to the Courts of Siam and Cochin China; Exhibiting a View of the Actual State of Those Kingdoms*. London: Henry Colburn and Richard Bentley.

Diagana, Melissa and Angres, Jyoti, 2013. *Fort Canning Hill: Exploring Singapore's Heritage And Nature*. USA: Oro Editions.

Dobbs, Stephen, 2003. *The Singapore River: A Social History, 1819-2002*. Singapore: NUS Press.

Glendinning, Victoria, 2012. *Raffles and the Golden Opportunity*. London: Profile Books.

Hall-Jones, John, 1971. *Mr Surveyor Thomson: Early days in Otago and Southland*. Wellington: Reed

Hall-Jones, John, & Hooi, Christopher, 1979. *An early surveyor in Singapore: John Turnbull Thomson in Singapore, 1841–1853*. Singapore: National Museum.

Hancock, T. H. H., 1986. *Coleman's Singapore*. Kuala Lumpur: The Malaysian Branch of The Royal Asiatic Society in association with Pelanduk Publications.

Hannigan, Tim, 2013. *Raffles and the British Invasion of Java*. Great Britain: Monsoon Books Pte. Ltd.

Holmes, Richard et al, 2002. *Romantics & Revolutionaries – Regency Portraits from the National Portrait Gallery, London*. London: National Portrait Gallery.

Hon, Joan, 1990. *Tidal Fortunes: A Story of Change: The Singapore River and Kallang Basin*. Singapore: Landmark Books

Hull, Sophia, 1830. *Memoir of the Life and Public Services of Sir Thomas Stamford Raffles, F.R.S. &c. Particularly in the Government of Java, 1811 – 1816, and of Bencoolen and its Dependencies, 1817 – 1824; with Details of the Commerce and Resources of the Eastern Archipelago, and Selections from his Correspondence*. London: John Murray.

Ibrahim Tahir (Ed.), 2013. *A Village Remembered: Kampong Radin Mas, 1800s–1973*. Singapore: OPUS Editorial Pte. Ltd.

Joshi, Yugal et al, 2012. "Cleaning of the Singapore River and Kallang Basin in Singapore: Economic, social and environmental dimensions." In *International Journal of Water Resources Development*. 28(4), 1-1, p. 2. Singapore: Lee Kuan Yew School of Public Policy. Available at: http://lkyspp2.nus.edu.sg/iwp/wp-content/uploads/sites/3/2013/04/Cleaning-of-the-Singapore-River_Intl-Journal-Wtr.pdf.

Koh, Audrey and Budi Wijaya, 2011. *INSITU Fort Canning Hill*. Singapore: Beautiful/Banal.

Koh, Buck Song, 2011. *Brand Singapore: How Nation Branding Built Asia's Leading Global City*. Singapore: Marshall Cavendish.

Koh, Qi Rui Vincent and Chew, Valerie, 2014. "Horsburgh Lighthouse" *Singapore Infopedia*. Singapore: National Library Board. Available at: http://eresources.nlb.gov.sg/infopedia/articles/SIP_107_2005-01-20.html?s=horsburgh%20lighthouse.

Lai, Chee Kien, 2016. "The Padang: Centrepiece of Colonial Design." *Biblioasia* Vol 12 Issue 3, Sep 8 2016. Singapore: National Library Board.

Lee, Olive, 1980. *Radin Mas: Folktale from Singapore*. Singapore: Spectrum Pub in association with Toppan.

Linehan, W., 1969. "The kings of 14th century Singapore". In *Journal of the Malaysian Branch of the Royal Asiatic Society*, Singapore 150th Anniversary Commemorative Issue, July 1969, 42 (1) (215), pp. 53 - 62. Retrieved from JSTOR. Available at: https://www.jstor.org/stable/41491965?seq=1#page_scan_tab_contents.

Marsita Omar, 2006. "Keramat Radin Mas" *Singapore Infopedia*. Singapore: National Library Board. Available at: http://eresources.nlb.gov.sg/infopedia/articles/SIP_1079_2010-05-27.html?s=raden%20mas.

McMurray, C., 2014. "The history of Fort Canning Hill." In *Passage*. Singapore: Friends of the Museums. Available at: http://www.fom.sg/Passage/2014/01FortCanning.pdf.

Munoz, P. M., 2006. *Early kingdoms of the Indonesian Archipelago and the Malay Peninsula*. Singapore: Editions Didier Millet.

National Heritage Board, 2016. "Clemenceau Bridge" *Roots.sg*. Singapore: National Heritage Board. Available at: https://roots.sg/Content/Places/landmarks/singapore-river-walk/clemenceau-bridge.

National Heritage Board, 2016. "Former Convent of the Holy Infant Jesus and Caldwell House." *Roots.sg*. Singapore: National Heritage Board. Available at: https://roots.sg/Content/Places/national-monuments/former-convent-of-the-holy-infant-jesus-chapel-and-caldwell-house-now-chijmes.

National Heritage Board, 2016. "Former Fullerton Building." *Roots.sg*. Singapore: National Heritage Board. Available at: https://roots.sg/Content/Places/national-monuments/former-fullerton-building.

National Heritage Board, 2016. "Historic Bridges Over the Singapore River." *Roots.sg*. Singapore: National Heritage Board. Available at: https://roots.sg/learn/resources/virtual-tours/historic-bridges-over-singapore-river.

National Heritage Board, 2018. *Singapore Trails – Singapore River Walk & Jubilee Walk*. Singapore: Straits Times Press and National Heritage Board.

National Library Board, 2015. *Visualising space: maps of Singapore and the region: collections from the National Library and National Archives of Singapore*. Singapore: National Library Board. Available at: http://www.nas.gov.sg/blogs/offtherecord/wp-content/uploads/2016/06/Visualising-Space_Ch3.-Mapping-Singapore-1819-2014-by-Mr-Mok-Ly-Yng.pdf.

Nor Afidah Abd Rahman, 2016. "Sang Nila Utama" *Singapore Infopedia*. Singapore: National Library Board. Available at: http://eresources.nlb.gov.sg/infopedia/articles/SIP_93_2005-01-26.html.

Oral History Department, 1986. *Singapore Lifeline: The River and its People*. Singapore: Times Books International.

Port of Singapore Authority, 1984. *Singapore: Portrait of a Port: A Pictorial History of the Port and Harbour of Singapore 1819–1984*. Singapore: Port Authority of Singapore.

Raffles, Thomas Stamford, 1830. *The History of Java. Volume I and II. Second Edition*. London: John Murray.

Renuka M, Ong, Eng Chuan and Loh, Pei Ying, 2016. "Former Asia Insurance Building (Ascott Raffles Place)." *Singapore Infopedia*. Singapore: National Library Board. Available at: http://eresources.nlb.gov.sg/infopedia/articles/SIP_592_2005-01-17.html?s=HSBC%20Building.

Sim, Cheryl, 2016. "John Turnbull Thomson." *Singapore Infopedia*. Singapore: National Library Board. Available at: http://eresources.nlb.gov.sg/infopedia/articles/SIP_818_2005-01-22.html?s=john%20turnbull%20thoson.

Tan, Audrey and Au-yong, Rachel, 2013. "Radin Mas: Legacy of a Princess." In *The Straits Times*. 9 September 2013.

Tan, Bonny, 2016. "Raffles Town Plan (Jackson Plan)" *Singapore Infopedia*. Singapore: National Library Board. Available at: http://eresources.nlb.gov.sg/infopedia/articles/SIP_658_2005-01-07.html?s=jackson%20plan.

Tiffin, Sarah, 2017. *Southeast Asia in Ruins: Art and Empire in the Early 19th Century*. Singapore: NUS Press.

Urban Redevelopment Authority, 2013. *Historic Waterfront*. Singapore: Urban Redevelopment Authority. Available at: https://www.ura.gov.sg/Conservation-Portal/Resources/Articles?bldg-id=CLIFFPR

Wright, Nadia H., 2017. *William Farquhar and Singapore: Stepping Out From Raffles' Shadow*. Penang: Entrepot Publishing.

MONUMENTS & ARCHITECTURE

Beamish, Jane and Ferguson, Jane, 1985. *A History of Singapore Architecture - The Making of a City*. Singapore: Graham Brash (Pte.) Ltd.

Benton, Charlotte, Benton, Tim and Wood, Ghislaine, (Eds.), 2003. *Art Deco, 1910 – 1939*. London: Victoria & Albert Museum.

Chan, Fook Weng, 2014. "Formation of Raffles Library and Museum (1974)." *Singapore Infopedia*. Singapore: National Library Board. Available at: http://eresources.nlb.gov.sg/infopedia/articles/SIP_690_2005-01-20.html?s=raffles%20library%20and%20museum.

Chan, Fook Weng, 2016. "Raffles Library and Museum building (1887 – 1960)." *Singapore Infopedia*. Singapore: National Library Board. Available at: http://eresources.nlb.gov.sg/infopedia/articles/SIP_254_2005-01-24.html?s=raffles%20library%20and%20museum.

Chew, Melanie, 2001. *Memories of the Fullerton*. Singapore: The Fullerton Hotel.

Chia, Yeong Jia Joshua and Tay, Shereen, 2016. "John Little." *Singapore Infopedia*. Singapore: National Library Board. Available at: http://eresources.nlb.gov.sg/infopedia/articles/SIP_1116_2010-06-14.html.

Chua, Alvin, 2011. "Overseas Union Bank." *Singapore Infopedia*. Singapore: National Library Board. Available at: http://eresources.nlb.gov.sg/infopedia/articles/SIP_1787_2011-02-24.html.

Chua, Alvin, 2011. "Tiong Bahru." *Singapore Infopedia*. Singapore: National Library Board. Available at: http://eresources.nlb.gov.sg/infopedia/articles/SIP_1700_2010-08-11.html.

Cornelius, Vernon, 1999. "Raffles Place." *Singapore Infopedia*. Singapore: National Library Board. Available at: http://eresources.nlb.gov.sg/infopedia/articles/SIP_864_2004-12-30.html?s=raffles%20place.

Cornelius, Vernon and Tan, Joanna H. S., 2011. "Former Supreme Court Building." *Singapore Infopedia*. Singapore: National Library Board. Available at: http://eresources.nlb.gov.sg/infopedia/articles/SIP_774_2005-01-10.html?s=old%20supreme%20court.

Cornelius-Takahama, Vernon, 2015. "Fullerton Building." *Singapore Infopedia*. Singapore: National Library Board. Available at: http://eresources.nlb.gov.sg/infopedia/articles/SIP_523_2005-01-19.html?s=fullerton.

Cornelius-Takahama, Vernon, 2015. "MPH." *Singapore Infopedia*. Singapore: National Library Board. Available at: http://eresources.nlb.gov.sg/infopedia/articles/SIP_61_2004-12-27.html?s=MPH%20Building.

Cornelius-Takahama, Vernon and Tan, Joanna H. S., 2010. "St Andrew's Cathedral." *Singapore Infopedia*. Singapore: National Library Board. Available at: http://eresources.nlb.gov.sg/infopedia/articles/SIP_25_2_2008-12-01.html?s=st%20andrews%20cathedral.

Cornelius-Takahama, Vernon and Ong,

Eng Chuan, 2006. "Cathay Building." *Singapore Infopedia*. Singapore: National Library Board. Available at: http://eresources.nlb.gov.sg/infopedia/articles/SIP_532_2004-12-17.html.

Davison, Julian, 2006. *Black & White – The Singapore House, 1898 - 1941*. Singapore: Talisman Publishing.

Davison, Julian, 2011. *Singapore Shophouse*. Singapore: Talisman Publishing.

Davison, Julian, 2018. *Swan & MacLaren – A Story of Singapore Architecture*. USA: Oro Editions.

Davison, Julian, 2018. "Chinese Renaissance Architecture." In *Biblioasia*, Volume 14 Issue 01. Singapore: National Library Board.

Doggett, Marjorie, 1957. *Characters of Light: A Guide to the Buildings of Singapore*. Singapore: Donald Moore.

Edwards, Norman, 1990. *The Singapore House and Residential Life, 1819 – 1939*. Singapore: Oxford University Press.

Heng, Chye Kiang and Yeo, Su-Jan, 2017. *Singapore Chronicles: URBAN PLANNING*. Singapore: Institute of Policy Studies and Straits Times Press.

Ho, Weng Hin, Naidu, Dinesh and Tan, Kar Lin, 2013. *Our Modern Past – Volume 1: A Visual Survey of Singapore Architecture, 1920s–70s*. Singapore: Singapore Heritage Society.

Kang, Ger-Wen, 2013. *Decoration and Symbolism in Chinese Architecture*. Singapore: Preservation of Sites and Monuments.

Koh, Lay Tin, 2010. "The Arts House (Old Parliament House)." *Singapore Infopedia*. Singapore: National Library Board. Available at: http://eresources.nlb.gov.sg/infopedia/articles/SIP_836_2005-01-06.html?s=old%20parliament%20house.

Lee, Kip Lin, 2015. *The Singapore House, 1819 – 1942*. Singapore: Marshall Cavendish Editions.

Lim, Irene and Lim, Fiona, 2015.

"Clifford Pier." *Singapore Infopedia*. Singapore: National Library Board. Available at: http://eresources.nlb.gov.sg/infopedia/articles/SIP_12_2004-12-14.html?s=clifford%20pier.

Liu, Gretchen, 1984. *Pastel Portraits: Singapore's Architectural Heritage*. Singapore: Singapore Coordinating Committee.

Liu, Gretchen, 1987. *One Hundred Years of the National Museum: Singapore 1887 – 1987*. Singapore: National Museum.

Liu, Gretchen, 1992. *Raffles Hotel*. Singapore: Landmark Books.

Liu, Gretchen, 1996. *In Granite and Chunam – National Monuments of Singapore*. Singapore: Landmark Books and Preservation of Monuments Board.

Marsita Omar, 2016. "Former Empress Place Building." *Singapore Infopedia*. Singapore: National Library Board. Available at: http://eresources.nlb.gov.sg/infopedia/articles/SIP_1132_2006-04-05.html.

National Heritage Board, 2013. *Tiong Bahru Heritage Trail*. Singapore: National Heritage Board. Available at: https://roots.sg/visit/trails/tiong-bahru-heritage-trail.

National Heritage Board, 2016. "Chesed-El Synagogue." *Roots.sg*. Singapore: National Heritage Board. Available at: https://roots.sg/Content/Places/national-monuments/chesed-el-synagogue.

National Heritage Board, 2016. "Chinese High School Clock Tower Building." *Roots.sg*. Singapore: National Heritage Board. Available at: https://roots.sg/Content/Places/national-monuments/chinese-high-school-clock-tower-building.

National Heritage Board, 2016. "Former Cathay Building." *Roots.sg*. Singapore: National Heritage Board. Available at: https://roots.sg/Content/Places/national-monuments/former-cathay-building-now-the-cathay.

National Heritage Board, 2016. "Former City Hall." *Roots.sg*. Singapore: National Heritage Board. Available at: https://roots.sg/Roots/Content/Places/national-monuments/former-city-hall.

National Heritage Board, 2016. "Former Empress Place Building (now Asian Civilisations Museum)." *Roots.sg*. Singapore: National Heritage Board. Available at: https://roots.sg/Content/Places/national-monuments/former-empress-place-building-now-asian-civilisations-museum.

National Heritage Board, 2016. "Former Parliament House and Annex Building (now Arts House)." *Roots.sg*. Singapore: National Heritage Board. Available at: https://roots.sg/Content/Places/national-monuments/former-parliament-house-and-annex-building-now-the-arts-house.

National Heritage Board, 2016. "Former Supreme Court." *Roots.sg*. Singapore: National Heritage Board. Available at: https://roots.sg/Content/Places/national-monuments/former-supreme-court.

National Heritage Board, 2016. "Former Tanjong Pagar Railway Station." *Roots.sg*. Singapore: National Heritage Board. Available at: https://roots.sg/Content/Places/national-monuments/former-tanjong-pagar-railway-station.

National Heritage Board, 2016. "Goodwood Park Hotel (Tower Block)." *Roots.sg*. Singapore: National Heritage Board. Available at: https://roots.sg/Content/Places/national-monuments/goodwood-park-hotel-tower-block.

National Heritage Board, 2016. "Johnston's and Clifford Pier." *Roots.sg*. Singapore: National Heritage Board. Available at: https://roots.sg/learn/stories/johnstons-and-clifford-pier/story.

National Heritage Board, 2016. "National Museum of Singapore." *Roots.sg*. Singapore: National Heritage Board. Available at: https://roots.sg/Content/Places/national-monuments/national-museum-of-singapore.

National Heritage Board, 2016. "Raffles Hotel." *Roots.sg*. Singapore: National Heritage Board. Available at: https://roots.sg/Content/Places/national-monuments/raffles-hotel.

National Heritage Board, 2016. "Raffles Place." *Roots.sg*. Singapore: National Heritage Board. Available at: https://roots.sg/Content/Places/historic-sites/raffles-place.

National Heritage Board, 2016. "St Andrew's Cathedral." *Roots.sg*. Singapore: National Heritage Board. Available at: https://roots.sg/Content/Places/national-monuments/saint-andrews-cathedral.

National Heritage Board, 2016. "Sultan Mosque." *Roots.sg*. Singapore: National Heritage Board. Available at: https://roots.sg/Content/Places/national-monuments/sultan-mosque.

National Heritage Board, 2016. "Telok Ayer Chinese Methodist Church." *Roots.sg*. Singapore: National Heritage Board. Available at: https://roots.sg/Content/Places/national-monuments/telok-ayer-chinese-methodist-church.

National Heritage Board, 2016. "The Majestic Theatre and Nam Tin Building (now Yue Hwa Building) on Eu Tong Sen Street." *Roots.sg*. Singapore: National Heritage Board. Available at: https://roots.sg/learn/collections/listing/1129531.

National Heritage Board, 2016. "The Union Building and the Hong Kong and Shanghai Bank Building." *Roots.sg*. Singapore: National Heritage Board. Available at: https://roots.sg/learn/collections/listing/1123177.

National Heritage Board, 2016. "Victoria Theatre and Victoria Concert Hall." *Roots.sg*. Singapore: National Heritage Board. Available at: https://roots.sg/Content/Places/national-monuments/victoria-theatre-and-concert-hall.

Ong, Christopher, 2016. "Swan & Maclaren." *Singapore Infopedia*. Singapore: National Library Board. Available at: http://eresources.nlb.gov.sg/infopedia/articles/SIP_1478_2009-02-26.html.

Preservation of Sites and Monuments, 2015. "National Museum of Singapore." *Singapore Infopedia*. Singapore: National Library Board. Available at: http://eresources.nlb.gov.sg/infopedia/articles/SIP_2015-08-31_132917.html?s=national%20gallery.

Preservation of Sites and Monuments, 2016. "Former City Hall." *Singapore Infopedia*. Singapore: National Library Board. Available at: http://eresources.nlb.gov.sg/infopedia/articles/SIP_849_2004-12-17.html?s=former%20city%20hall.

Swan & Maclaren. (2013–2014). *History*. Retrieved October 13 2016 from Swan & Maclaren website. Available at: http://www.swanmaclaren.com/2014/history.php.

Tan, Annette and Koh, Yuen Lin, 2015. *Fullerton Stories – Rediscovering Singapore's Heritage*. Singapore: Gatehouse Publishing.

Tan, Bonny, 2015. "Dalhousie Obelisk." *Singapore Infopedia*. Singapore: National Library Board. Available at: http://eresources.nlb.gov.sg/infopedia/articles/SIP_481_2005-01-20.html?s=Dalhousie%20obelisk.

Tan, Bonny, 2015. "Stamford House." *Singapore Infopedia*. Singapore: National Library Board. Available at: http://eresources.nlb.gov.sg/infopedia/articles/SIP_925_2005-01-27.html?s=stamford%20house.

Tan Bonny, 2016. "Victoria Theatre and Concert Hall." *Singapore Infopedia*. Singapore: National Library Board. Available at: http://eresources.nlb.gov.sg/infopedia/articles/SIP_770_2004-12-16.html?s=victoria%20memorial%20hall.

Tan, Joanna H. S., 2016. "Raffles Hotel." *Singapore Infopedia*. Singapore: National Library Board. Available at: http://eresources.nlb.gov.sg/infopedia/articles/SIP_37_2005-01-05.html?s=raffles%20hotel.

Vina, Jie-Min Prasad and Jaime Koh, 2014. "Raffles Institution." *Singapore Infopedia*. Singapore: National Library

Board. Available at: http://eresources.nlb.gov.sg/infopedia/articles/SIP_17_2004-12-21.html?s=raffles%20institution.

Wijeysingha, Eugene, 1989. *The Eagle Breeds A Gryphon – The Story of Raffles Institution, 1823 – 1985*. Singapore: Pioneer Book Centre.

Yew, Guan Pak Peter, 2016. "Robinsons Department Store." *Singapore Infopedia*. Singapore: National Library Board. Available at: http://eresources.nlb.gov.sg/infopedia/articles/SIP_561_2005-01-25.html.

CULTURES & COMMUNITIES

Abdul Jalal Ajmain et al, 1960. *Adat Melayu*. Singapore: Educational Book Centre.

Ahmed Ibrahim, Abhushouk and Ahmed Ibrahim, Hassan (Eds.), 2009. *The Hadhrami Diaspora in Southeast Asia – Identity Maintenance or Assimilation?* Leiden: Koninklijke Brill NV.

Alatas, Syed Farid (Ed.), 2010. *Hadhramaut Arabs Across the Indian Ocean – Contributions to Southeast Asian Economy and Society*. Singapore: National Library Board.

Arasaratnam, Sinappah, 1966. *Indian Festivals in Malaya*. Kuala Lumpur: Department of Indian Studies, University of Malaya.

AsiaPac Editorial, 2012. *Celebrate Chinese Culture: Chinese Auspicious Culture*. Singapore: AsiaPac Books and Foreign Language Press.

Azrah, Edian and Tan, Joanna, 2016. "Hajjah Fatimah Mosque." *Singapore Infopedia*. Singapore: National Library Board. Available at: http://eresources.nlb.gov.sg/infopedia/articles/SIP_259_2005-01-06.html?s=hajjah%20fatimah%20mosque.

Berry, Graham, 2015. *From Kilts to Sarongs – Scottish Pioneers of Singapore*. Singapore: Landmark Books.

Bieder, Joan, 2007. *The Jews of Singapore*.

Singapore: Suntree Media Private Limited.

Bowen, H. V., McAleer, John and Blyth, Robert J., 2011. *Monsoon Traders – The Maritime World of the East India Company*. London: Scala Publishers and the National Maritime Museum.

Braga-Blake, Myrna, 1992. *Singapore Eurasians – Memories and Hopes*. Singapore: Times Editions and The Eurasian Association.

Cheah, Hwei-Fen, 2017. *Nyonya Needlework – Embroidery and Beadwork in the Peranakan World*. Exhibition Catalogue. Singapore: Asian Civilisations Museum.

Chia, Felix, 1980. *The Babas*. 2014 Edition. Singapore: Landmark Books.

Chia, Joshua Yeong Jia, 2006. "Teutonia Club." *Singapore Infopedia*. Singapore: National Library Board. Available at: http://eresources.nlb.gov.sg/infopedia/articles/SIP_1168_2009-02-13.html?s=travellers%20palm.

Chia, Joshua Yeong Jia, 2007. "Old Sea View Hotel." *Singapore Infopedia*. Singapore: National Library Board. Available at: http://eresources.nlb.gov.sg/infopedia/articles/SIP_1181_2007-08-29.html.

Chia, Joshua Yeong Jia, 2016. "Abraham Solomon." *Singapore Infopedia*. Singapore: National Library Board. Available at: http://eresources.nlb.gov.sg/infopedia/articles/SIP_1205_2008-12-06.html.

Chia, Joshua and Tan, Bonny, 2010. "Singapore Recreation Club." *Singapore Infopedia*. Singapore: National Library Board. Available at: http://eresources.nlb.gov.sg/infopedia/articles/SIP_1041_2010-05-07.html.

Chia, Philip, 2012. *Singapore Heritage Cookbook: Peranakan Heritage Cooking*. Singapore: Marshall-Cavendish Cuisine.

Chong, Alan et al, 2015. *Great Peranakans – Fifty Remarkable Lives*. Exhibition Catalogue. Singapore: Asian Civilisations Museum.

Chua, Alvin, 2012. "Joo Chiat." *Singapore Infopedia*. Singapore: National Library Board. Available at: http://eresources.nlb.gov.sg/infopedia/articles/SIP_946__2008-11-13.html?s=joo%20chiat.

Cornelius, Vernon, 1999. "Bras Basah Road." *Singapore Infopedia*. Singapore: National Library Board. Available at: http://eresources.nlb.gov.sg/infopedia/articles/SIP_227_2005-01-25.html.

Cornelius, Vernon, 2016. "Tanjong Katong." *Singapore Infopedia*. Singapore: National Library Board. Available at: http://eresources.nlb.gov.sg/infopedia/articles/SIP_829_2005-01-18.html?s=katong.

Cornelius-Takahama, Vernon, 2016. "Masjid Omar Kampong Melaka." *Singapore Infopedia*. Singapore: National Library Board. Available at: http://eresources.nlb.gov.sg/infopedia/articles/SIP_688_2004-12-27.html.

Cornelius-Takahama, Vernon and Tan, Joanna, 2016. "Jamae Mosque." *Singapore Infopedia*. Singapore: National Library Board. Available at: http://eresources.nlb.gov.sg/infopedia/articles/SIP_520_2004-12-16.html?s=jamae%20mosque.

Daus, Ronald, 1989. *Portuguese Eurasian Commmunities in Southeast Asia*. Singapore: Institute of Southeast Asian Studies.

De Camões, Luís Vaz, 1572. *Os Lusíadas*. Project Gutenberg Edition. Available at: http://www.gutenberg.org/ebooks/3333.

Dhoraisingam, Samuel S., 2006. *Peranakan Indians of Singapore and Melaka: Indian Babas and Nonyas – Chitty Melaka*. Singapore: Institute of Southeast Asian Studies.

Edwards, Norman, 1991. *The Singapore House and Residential Life, 1819 – 1939*. 2017 Edition. Singapore: Talisman Publishing.

Ee, Randall et al, 2017. *Peranakan Museum Guide (Revised)*. Singapore: Asian Civilisations Museum.

Foo, Su Ling, Lim, Chen Sian, Sheau, Theng Wee and Yeo, Kang Shua, 2017. *NUS Baba House: Architecture and Artefacts of a Straits Chinese Home.* Singapore: Editions Didier Millet.

Goh, Pei Kii, (Ed.), 1997. *Origins of Chinese Festivals.* Singapore: Asiapac.

Goodwood Park Hotel, 2000. *Goodwood Park Hotel (1900 – 2000) – 100 Years of Hospitality.* Singapore: Goodwood Park Hotel.

Guleij Ron and Knapp, Gerritt (Eds.), 2017. *The Dutch East India Company Book.* The Netherlands: WBooks and Nationaal Archief.

Hamilton, A. W., 1944. *Malay Pantuns. 2010 Edition.* UK: Neilson Press.

Ho, Stephanie, 2014. "Deepavali." *Singapore Infopedia.* Singapore: National Library Board. Available at: http://eresources.nlb.gov.sg/infopedia/articles/SIP_559_2005-01-04.html?s=deepavali.

Hutton, Wendy, 2007. *Singapore Food.* Singapore: Marshall Cavendish Cuisine.

Inter-Religious Organisation Singapore, 2018. *Website.* Singapore: Inter-Religious Organisation Singapore. Available at: www.iro.sg.

Jonas, Patrick, 2017. "The man behind fish head curry." In *The Straits Times,* 10 December 2017. Online version available at: https://www.straitstimes.com/singapore/the-man-behind-fish-head-curry.

Kanga, Suna and Khaneja, Subina, 2017. *The Parsis of Singapore – History, Culture, Cuisine.* Singapore: Epigram Books.

Kee, Ming-Yuet, 2017. *Peranakan Chinese Porcelain – Vibrant Festive Ware of the Straits Chinese.* Singapore: Tuttle Publishing.

Koh, Jaime, 2013. "Hari Raya Haji." *Singapore Infopedia.* Singapore: National Library Board. Available at: http://eresources.nlb.gov.sg/infopedia/articles/SIP_694__2009-01-02.html?s=hari%20raya%20puasa.

Kuo, Eddie C. Y. and Chan, Brenda, 2016. *Singapore Chronicles: LANGUAGE.* Singapore: Institute of Policy Studies and Straits Times Press.

Lai, Ah Eng, 2017. *Singapore Chronicles: RELIGION.* Singapore: Institute of Policy Studies and Straits Times Press.

Lau, Aileen T. and Platzdash, Bernhard (Eds.), 2010. *Malay Heritage of Singapore.* Singapore: Suntree Media Private Limited, in association with Malay Heritage Foundation, Singapore.

Lee, Edwin, 1991. *The British as Rulers: Governing Multi-racial Singapore, 1867 – 1914.* Singapore: Singapore University Press, National University of Singapore.

Lee, Geok Boi, 2002. *The Religious Monuments of Singapore – Faiths of our Forefathers.* Singapore: Landmark Books.

Lee, Peter et al, 2016. *Port Cities – Multicultural Emporiums of Asia, 1500 – 1900.* Exhibition Catalogue. Singapore: Asian Civilisations Museum.

Lim, Edmund W. K. and Kho, Ee Moi, 2005. *The Chesed-El Synagogue: its History and People.* Singapore: Trustees of Chesed-El Synagogue.

Lim, Gillian and Neo, Tiong Seng, 2016. "St Joseph's Church (Portuguese Mission)." *Singapore Infopedia.* Singapore: National Library Board. Available at: http://eresources.nlb.gov.sg/infopedia/articles/SIP_1707_2010-09-02.html?s=saint%20josephs%20church.

Lim, Rosemary, 2008. *An Irish Tour of Singapore.* Singapore: Two Trees Private Limited.

Lingner, Richard and Onn, Clement (Eds), 2017. *ACM Treasures – Collection Highlights.* Singapore: Asian Civilisations Museum.

Lip, Evelyn, 1985. *Chinese Beliefs and Superstitions.* Singapore: Graham Brash.

Lowe-Ismail, Geraldene, 1998. *Chinatown Memories.* Singapore: Talisman Publishing.

Keay, John, 1991. *The Honourable Company – A History of the English East India Company.* New York: MacMillan Publishing Company.

Kong, Lily, and Chang, T. C., 2001. *Joo Chiat: A Living Legacy.* Singapore: Joo Chiat Citizens' Consultative Committee in association with National Archives of Singapore.

Kua, Bak Lim, (Ed.), 2014. *Singapore Chinese – Then and Now.* Singapore: Singapore Federation of Chinese Clan Associations.

Manmatha Nath Dutt (Ed.), 1891. *The Ramayana – Translated into English Prose from the Original Sanskrit of Valmiki.* Calcutta: Girish Chandra Chackravarti.

Mazlan Anuar and Heirwin Mohd Nasir, 2018. "Hari Raya Puasa." *Singapore Infopedia.* Singapore: National Library Board. Available at: http://eresources.nlb.gov.sg/infopedia/articles/SIP_919_2004-12-20.html?s=hari%20raya%20puasa.

McGuigan, Debra Lynn, 1995. "The Borobudur, Central Java ca. 732-910 A.D.". In *Canadian Journal of Netherlandic Studies.* Issue XVI, Vol ii, Fall 1995, pgs 5 – 18. Toronto: University of Toronto.

Morley, J. A. E., 1949. "The Arabs and the Eastern Trade." In *Journal of the Malayan Branch of the Royal Asiatic Society.* 22(1), 155. Retrieved from JSTOR via NLB's eResources website. Available at: http://eresources.nlb.gov.sg/.

Mowe, Rosalind (Ed.), 1999. *Southeast Asian Specialities – A Culinary Journey through Singapore, Malaysia and Indonesia.* Singapore: Konemann.

Mukunthan, Michael and Nor Afidah Abd Rahman, 2016. "Syed Omar Aljunied." *Singapore Infopedia.* Singapore: National Library Board. Available at: http://eresources.nlb.gov.sg/infopedia/articles/SIP_847_2004-12-29.html?s=aljunied.

Naidu, Thulaja, 2003. "Amoy Street." *Singapore Infopedia.* Singapore: National Library Board. Available at: http://eresources.nlb.gov.sg/infopedia/articles/

SIP_347_2004-12-24.html?s=amoy%20street.

Naidu, Thulaja, 2016. "David Elias Building." *Singapore Infopedia.* Singapore: National Library Board. Available at: http://eresources.nlb.gov.sg/infopedia/articles/SIP_274_2005-01-05.html?s=ellison%20building.

Naidu, Thulaja, 2016. "Jawi Peranakkan." *Singapore Infopedia.* Singapore: National Library Board. Available at: http://eresources.nlb.gov.sg/infopedia/articles/SIP_106_2005-02-02.html?s=jawi.

Naidu, Thulaja, 2016. "Sri Krishnan Temple." *Singapore Infopedia.* Singapore: National Library Board. Available at: http://eresources.nlb.gov.sg/infopedia/articles/SIP_276_2004-12-24.html?s=sri%20krishnan.

Naidu, Thulaja, 2016. "Yueh Hai Ching Temple." *Singapore Infopedia.* Singapore: National Library Board. Available at: http://eresources.nlb.gov.sg/infopedia/articles/SIP_327_2005-01-18.html?s=yueh%20hai%20ching.

Naidu, Thulaja, 2017. "Fuk Tak Chi Temple." *Singapore Infopedia.* Singapore: National Library Board. Available at: http://eresources.nlb.gov.sg/infopedia/articles/SIP_232_2004-12-10.html?s=fuk%20tak%20chi.

Naidu, Thulaja, 2018. "Kwan Im Thong Hood Cho Temple." *Singapore Infopedia.* Singapore: National Library Board. Available at: http://eresources.nlb.gov.sg/infopedia/articles/SIP_275_2005-01-03.html?s=kwan%20im%20thong%20hood%20cho.

Nuradilah Ramlan and Neo, Tiong Seng, 2016. "Central Sikh Temple." *Singapore Infopedia.* Singapore: National Library Board. Available at: http://eresources.nlb.gov.sg/infopedia/articles/SIP_1721_2010-11-09.html?s=central%20sikh%20temple.

National Heritage Board, 2016. "Al-Abrar Mosque." *Roots.sg.* Singapore: National Heritage Board. Available at: https://roots.sg/Content/Places/national-monuments/al-abrar-mosque.

National Heritage Board, 2016. "Armenian Apostolic Church of Saint Gregory the Illuminator." *Roots.sg.* Singapore: National Heritage Board. Available at: https://roots.sg/Content/Places/national-monuments/armenian-apostolic-church-of-saint-gregory-the-illuminator.

National Heritage Board, 2016. "Cathedral of the Good Shepherd." *Roots.sg.* Singapore: National Heritage Board. Available at: https://roots.sg/Content/Places/national-monuments/cathedral-of-the-good-shepherd.

National Heritage Board, 2016. "Chesed-El Synagogue." *Roots.sg.* Singapore: National Heritage Board. Available at: https://roots.sg/Content/Places/national-monuments/chesed-el-synagogue.

National Heritage Board, 2016. "Church of Our Lady of Lourdes." *Roots.sg.* Singapore: National Heritage Board. Available at: https://roots.sg/Content/Places/national-monuments/church-of-our-lady-of-lourdes.

National Heritage Board, 2016. "Church of St Peter and Paul." *Roots.sg.* Singapore: National Heritage Board. Available at: https://roots.sg/Content/Places/national-monuments/church-of-st-peter-and-st-paul.

National Heritage Board, 2016. "Former Keng Teck Whay Building." *Roots.sg.* Singapore: National Heritage Board. Available at: https://roots.sg/Content/Places/national-monuments/former-keng-teck-whay-building.

National Heritage Board, 2016. "Former Nagore Durgah." *Roots.sg.* Singapore: National Heritage Board. Available at: https://roots.sg/Content/Places/national-monuments/former-nagore-dargah.

National Heritage Board, 2016. "Former St Joseph's Institution (now Singapore Art Museum)." *Roots.sg.* Singapore: National Heritage Board. Available at: https://roots.sg/Content/Places/national-monuments/former-saint-josephs-institution-now-singapore-art-museum.

National Heritage Board, 2016. "Fuk Tak Chi." *Roots.sg.* Singapore: National Heritage Board: Available at: https://roots.sg/Content/Places/historic-sites/fuk-tak-chi.

National Heritage Board, 2016. "Hajjah Fatimah Mosque." *Roots.sg.* Singapore: National Heritage Board: Available at: https://roots.sg/Content/Places/national-monuments/hajjah-fatimah-mosque.

National Heritage Board, 2016. "Istana Kampong Gelam." *Roots.sg.* Singapore: National Heritage Board. Available at: https://roots.sg/Content/Places/national-monuments/istana-kampong-glam.

National Heritage Board, 2016. "Jamae Mosque." *Roots.sg.* Singapore: National Heritage Board. Available at: https://roots.sg/Content/Places/national-monuments/jamae-mosque.

National Heritage Board, 2016. "Madrasah Alsagoff Al-Arabiah." *Roots.sg.* Singapore: National Heritage Board. Available at: https://roots.sg/Content/Places/surveyed-sites/alsagoff-arab-school.

National Heritage Board, 2016. "Maghain Aboth Synagogue." *Roots.sg.* Singapore: National Heritage Board: Available at: https://roots.sg/Content/Places/national-monuments/maghain-aboth-synagogue.

National Heritage Board, 2016. "Prinsep Street Presbyterian Church." *Roots.sg.* Singapore: National Heritage Board. Available at: https://roots.sg/Content/Places/national-monuments/prinsep-street-presbyterian-church.

National Heritage Board, 2016. "St Joseph's Church." *Roots.sg.* Singapore: National Heritage Board. Available at: https://roots.sg/Content/Places/national-monuments/st-josephs-church.

National Heritage Board, 2016. "Sri Mariamman Temple." *Roots.sg.* Singapore: National Heritage Board. Available at: https://roots.sg/Content/Places/national-monuments/sri-mariamman-temple.

National Heritage Board, 2016. "Sultan

Mosque." *Roots.sg*. Singapore: National Heritage Board. Available at: https://roots.sg/Content/Places/national-monuments/sultan-mosque.

National Heritage Board, 2016. "Telok Ayer: Street of Diversity." *Roots.sg*. Singapore: National Heritage Board. Available at: https://roots.sg/learn/stories/telok-ayer/story.

National Heritage Board, 2016. "Thian Hock Keng Temple." *Roots.sg*. Singapore: National Heritage Board. Available at: https://roots.sg/Content/Places/national-monuments/thian-hock-keng.

National Heritage Board, 2016. "Ying Fo Fui Kun." *Roots.sg*. Singapore: National Heritage Board. Available at: https://roots.sg/Content/Places/national-monuments/ying-fo-fui-kun.

National Heritage Board, 2016. "Yueh Hai Ching Temple." *Roots.sg*. Singapore: National Heritage Board. Available at: https://roots.sg/Content/Places/national-monuments/yueh-hai-ching-temple.

Noor Aishah Abdul Rahman, 2017. *Singapore Chronicles: MALAYS*. Singapore: Institute of Policy Studies and Straits Times Press.

Ong, Y. D., 2005. *Buddhism in Singapore – A Short Narrative History*. Singapore: Skylark Publications.

Pereira, Alexius A., 2015. *Singapore Chronicles: EURASIANS*. Singapore: Institute of Policy Studies and Straits Times Press.

Pereira, Quentin, 2012. *Singapore Heritage Cookbook: Eurasian Heritage Cooking*. Singapore: Marshall Cavendish Cuisine.

Pillai, Anita Devi and Arumugam, Puva, 2017. *From Kerala to Singapore – Voices from the Singapore Malayalee Community*. Singapore: Marshall Cavendish Editions.

Pilon, Maxime and Weiler, Daniele, 2011. *The French in Singapore – An Illustrated History (1819 – today)*. Singapore: Editions Didier Millet.

Rai, Rajesh, 2014. *Indians in Singapore*

1819 – 1945: Diaspora in the Colonial Port City. New Delhi: Oxford University Press.

Rai, Rajesh and A. Mani (Eds.), 2017. *Singapore Indian Heritage*. Singapore: Indian Heritage Centre.

Rakunathan Narayanan, 2016. "Pongal." *Singapore Infopedia*. Singapore: National Library Board. Available at: http://eresources.nlb.gov.sg/infopedia/articles/SIP_590_2004-12-28.html.

Renuka, M. and Rakunathan Narayanan, 2002. "Fish head curry." *Singapore Infopedia*. Singapore: National Library Board. Available at: http://eresources.nlb.gov.sg/infopedia/articles/SIP_624_2005-01-04.html?s=fish%20head%20curry.

Sanmugam, Devagi and Shanmugam Kasinathan, 2011. *Singapore Heritage Cookbook: Indian Heritage Cooking*. Singapore: Marshall Cavendish Cuisine.

Seow, Renee, 2013. "Alkaff Mansion." *Singapore Infopedia*. Singapore: National Library Board. Available at: http://eresources.nlb.gov.sg/infopedia/articles/SIP_2013-05-02_080502.html?s=alkaff.

Sharp, Ilsa, 2008. *The E & O Hotel – Pearl of Penang*. Singapore: Marshall Cavendish.

Shennan, Margaret, 2000. *Out in the Midday Sun – The British in Malaya 1880 – 1960. 2015 Edition*. Singapore: Monsoon Books.

Siddique, Sharon and Nirmala Puru Shotam, 1990. *Singapore's Little India – past, present, and future. Second Edition*. Singapore: Institute of Southeast Asian Studies.

Sim, Cheryl, 2014. "Zhong Yuan Jie (Hungry Ghost Festival)." *Singapore Infopedia*. Singapore: National Library Board. Available at: http://eresources.nlb.gov.sg/infopedia/articles/SIP_758_2004-12-16.html.

Singapore Federation of Chinese Clan Associations, 1989. *Chinese Customs and Festivals in Singapore*. Singapore:

Singapore Federation of Chinese Clan Associations.

Singapore Federation of Chinese Clan Associations, 1990. *Chinese Heritage*. Singapore: Singapore Federation of Chinese Clan Associations.

Singapore Recreation Club, 2008. *Singapore Recreation Club Celebrates 1883 – 2007*. Singapore: Singapore Recreation Club.

Sinha, Vineeta, 2015. *Singapore Chronicles: INDIANS*. Singapore: Institute of Policy Studies and Straits Times Press.

Song, Ong Siang, 1923. *One Hundred Years' History of the Chinese in Singapore. The Annotated 2016 Edition*. Singapore: National Library Board.

Stark, Freya, 1990. *The southern gates of Arabia: A journey in the Hadhramaut*. London: Arrow.

Suárez, Thomas, 1999. *Early Mapping of Southeast Asia*. Hong Kong: Periplus Editions.

Tan, Bonny, 1998. "Mid-autumn Festival (Zhong Qiu Jie)." *Singapore Infopedia*. Singapore: National Library Board. Available at: http://eresources.nlb.gov.sg/infopedia/articles/SIP_804_2005-01-13.html.

Tan, Bonny, 2000. "Chinese New Year customs in Singapore." *Singapore Infopedia*. Singapore: National Library Board. Available at: http://eresources.nlb.gov.sg/infopedia/articles/SIP_948__2009-01-02.html?s=chinese%20new%20year.

Tan, Bonny, 2009. "Syed Omar bin Mohammed Alsagoff." *Singapore Infopedia*. Singapore: National Library Board. Available at: http://eresources.nlb.gov.sg/infopedia/articles/SIP_1624_2009-12-31.html?s=alsagoff.

Tan, Bonny, 2010. "Thian Hock Keng." *Singapore Infopedia*. Singapore: National Library Board. Available at: http://eresources.nlb.gov.sg/infopedia/articles/SIP_793_2005-01-10.html?s=thian%20hock%20keng.

Tan, Bonny, 2013. "Teh tarik." *Singapore Infopedia*. Singapore: National Library Board. Available at: http://eresources.nlb.gov.sg/infopedia/articles/SIP_2013-07-19_103055.html?s=teh%20tarik.

Tan, Bonny, 2016. "Thaipusam." *Singapore Infopedia*. Singapore: National Library Board. Available at: http://eresources.nlb.gov.sg/infopedia/articles/SIP_760_2004-12-27.html.

Tan, Bonny, 2017. "Syed Omar bin Omar Alsagoff." *Singapore Infopedia*. Singapore: National Library Board. Available at: http://eresources.nlb.gov.sg/infopedia/articles/SIP_1623_2009-12-31.html?s=alsagoff.

Tan, Bonny and Marsita Omar, 2016. "Keramat Habib Noh." *Singapore Infopedia*. Singapore: National Library Board. Available at: http://eresources.nlb.gov.sg/infopedia/articles/SIP_1573_2009-09-25.html?s=habib%20noh.

Tan, Bonny and Chew, Valerie, 2010. "Manasseh Meyer." *Singapore Infopedia*. Singapore: National Library Board. Available at: http://eresources.nlb.gov.sg/infopedia/articles/SIP_830_2004-12-29.html.

Tan, Bonny and Chew, Valerie, 2016. "Sri Mariamman Temple." *Singapore Infopedia*. Singapore: National Library Board. Available at: http://eresources.nlb.gov.sg/infopedia/articles/SIP_778_2004-12-23.html?s=sri%20mariamman%20temple.

Tan, Bonny and Tan, Joanna H. S., Valerie, 2016. "Armenian Church." *Singapore Infopedia*. Singapore: National Library Board. Available at: http://eresources.nlb.gov.sg/infopedia/articles/SIP_809_2004-12-23.html?s=armenian%20church.

Tan, Christopher and Van, Amy, 2013. *Singapore Heritage Cookbook: Chinese Heritage Cooking*. Singapore: Marshall Cavendish Cuisine.

Tan, Sylvia, 2016. *Singapore Chronicles: FOOD*. Singapore: Institute of Policy Studies and Straits Times Press.

Tan, Thomas T. W. (Ed.), 1990. *Chinese Dialect Groups: Traits and Trades*. Singapore: Opinion Books.

Teng, Sharon, 2016. "Telok Ayer Street." *Singapore Infopedia*. Singapore: National Library Board. Available at: http://eresources.nlb.gov.sg/infopedia/articles/SIP_656_2004-12-31.html?s=telok%20ayer%20stret.

Tomlin, Jacob, 1831. *Journal of a Nine Months Residence in Siam*. London: Frederick Westley and A. H. Davis. E-book available at: https://books.google.dk/books?id=adWpS20yJJQC&printsec=frontcover&dq=jacob+tomlin+-+a+missionary+journal+kept+at+singapore+and+-siam+1832&hl=en&sa=X&ved=0ahUKEwiB5q2muLzbAhUFfy-wKHZU-AkIQ6AEIMjAC#v=onepage&q&f=false.

Urban Redevelopment Authority, 2016. *Chinatown Trail*. Singapore: Urban Redevelopment Authority. Available at: https://roots.sg/visit/trails/chinatown-trail.

Urban Redevelopment Authority, 2005. *Kampong Glam Trail*. Singapore: Urban Redevelopment Authority. Available at: https://roots.sg/visit/trails/kampong-glam-trail.

Usma, G. S. and Singh, D., (Eds.), 2008. *Sikhi – A Way of Life*. Singapore: Sikh Advisory Board.

Van Dyke, Paul A., 2007. *The Canton Trade – Life and Enterprise on the China Coast, 1700 – 1845*. Hong Kong: Hong Kong University Press.

Vasu, Suchittra, 2002. "Easter." *Singapore Infopedia*. Singapore: National Library Board. Available at: http://eresources.nlb.gov.sg/infopedia/articles/SIP_942_2004-12-30.html.

Vasu, Suchittra, 2002. "Hainanese Chicken Rice." *Singapore Infopedia*. Singapore: National Library Board. Available at: http://eresources.nlb.gov.sg/infopedia/articles/SIP_910_2005-01-11.html?s=hainanese%20chicken%20rice.

Vasu, Suchittra, 2015. "Theemithi." *Singapore Infopedia*. Singapore: National Library Board. Available at: http://eresources.nlb.gov.sg/infopedia/articles/SIP_762_2004-12-23.html.

Vasu, Suchittra, 2016. "Dragon Boat Festival." *Singapore Infopedia*. Singapore: National Library Board. Available at: http://eresources.nlb.gov.sg/infopedia/articles/SIP_67_2004-12-27.html.

Vasu, Suchittra, 2017. "Satay." *Singapore Infopedia*. Singapore: National Library Board. Available at: http://eresources.nlb.gov.sg/infopedia/articles/SIP_888_2005-01-10.html.

Vasu, Suchittra and Azrah, Edian, 2018. "Prophet Mohammed's Birthday." *Singapore Infopedia*. Singapore: National Library Board. Available at: http://eresources.nlb.gov.sg/infopedia/articles/SIP_323_2004-12-28.html?s=malud%20nabi.

Vasu, Suchittra and Pwee, Timothy, 2008. "Vesak Day." *Singapore Infopedia*. Singapore: National Library Board. Available at: http://eresources.nlb.gov.sg/infopedia/articles/SIP_242_2004-12-30.html?s=vesak%20day.

Vasu, Suchittra and Renuka, M., 1999. "Vesakhi (Sikh New Year)." *Singapore Infopedia*. Singapore: National Library Board. Available at: http://eresources.nlb.gov.sg/infopedia/articles/SIP_755_2004-12-30.html?s=vesakhi.

Wang, Gungwu, 2003. *The Nanhai Trade – Early Chinese Trade in the South China Sea*. Singapore: Eastern Universities Press.

Wee, Peter, 2009. *A Peranakan Legacy – The Heritage of the Straits Chinese*. Singapore: Marshall Cavendish Editions.

Wright, Nadia H., 2003. *Respected Citizens – The History of the Armenians in Singapore and Malaysia*. Australia: Amassia Publishing.

Zahara, Rita, 2012. *Singapore Heritage Cookbook: Malay Heritage Cooking*. Singapore: Marshall Cavendish Cuisine.

Arts & Leisure

Achjadi, Judi and H. Santosa Doellah, 2011. *The Glory of Batik: The Danar Hadi Collection.* Singapore: Tuttle Publishing.

Bharata Muni, 500 BCE. *The Natyasastra – A Treatise on Hindu Dramaturgy and Histrionics.* Translated from Sanskrit by Manomohan Ghosh in 1951. Calcutta: Asiatic Society of Bengal.

Cai, Serene, 2011. "Wayang (Chinese Street Opera)." *Singapore Infopedia.* Singapore: National Library Board. Available at: http://eresources.nlb.gov.sg/infopedia/articles/SIP_1218_2011-06-28.html?s=chinese%20wayang.

Chen, Wen-Hsi, 1987. *Chen Wen Hsi – Paintings.* Singapore: Old & New Gallery.

Chia, Jane, 1997. *Georgette Chen.* Singapore: Singapore Art Museum.

Chong, Alan and Murphy, Stephen (Eds.), 2017. *The Tang Shipwreck – Art and Exchange in the 9th Century.* Singapore: Asian Civilisations Museum.

Creamer, Ruth, 2018. "Georgette Chen." *Singapore Infopedia.* Singapore: National Library Board. Available at: http://eresources.nlb.gov.sg/infopedia/articles/SIP_698_2005-01-12.html?s=nanyang%20style.

Fadzillah binti A. Rahim, 2007. *Styles of Jawi Scripts of the Early Malay Manuscripts (16th – 20th century).* Kuala Lumpur: Thinkers' Library.

Fleischmann-Heck, Isa et al, 2007. *Batik: 75 Selected Masterpieces – the Rudolf G. Smend Collection.* Singapore: Tuttle Publishing.

Gardner, Gerald B., 1936. *Keris and Other Malay Weapons.* PDF Edition. Singapore: Progressive Publishing Company. Available at: http://www.wicca.pl/MalayWeapons.pdf.

Ho, Stephanie, 2015. "Chen Wen Hsi." *Singapore Infopedia.* Singapore: National Library Board. Available at: http://eresources.nlb.gov.sg/infope-dia/articles/SIP_772_2004-12-29.html?s=nanyang%20style.

Hudson, Herbert H., 1892. *The Malay Orthography.* PDF Edition. Singapore: Kelly & Walsh, Limited. Available at: https://ia802609.us.archive.org/0/items/malayorthography00hudsrich/malayorthography00hudsrich.pdf.

Kerlogue, Fiona and Sosrowardoyo, Tara, 2004. *Batik – Design, Style & History.* London: Thames & Hudson.

Koh, Jaime, 2013. "Baju kurong." *Singapore Infopedia.* Singapore: National Library Board. Available at: http://eresources.nlb.gov.sg/infopedia/articles/SIP_2013-09-06_173434.html?s=sarong.

Kwok, Kian Chow, 1996. *Channels & Confluences – A History of Singapore Art.* Singapore: Singapore Art Museum.

Lee, Chor Lin, 2007. *Batik – Creating An Identity. 2nd Edition.* Singapore: Editions Didier Millet.

Lee, Meiyu, 2016. "Dragon dance." *Singapore Infopedia.* Singapore: National Library Board. Available at: http://eresources.nlb.gov.sg/infopedia/articles/SIP_924_2004-12-30.html.

Lee, Peter, 2014. *Sarong Kebaya – Peranakan Fashion in an Interconnected World, 1500 – 1950.* Singapore: Asian Civilisations Museum.

Lee, Tong Soon, 2008. *Chinese Street Opera in Singapore.* Illinois: University of Illinois Press.

Liu, Gretchen, and Phillips, Angelina (Eds.), 1988. *Wayang – A History of Chinese Street Opera in Singapore.* Singapore: National Archives of Singapore.

Low, Sze Wee and Cai, Heng, 2017. *Strokes of Life – The Art of Chen Chong Swee.* Singapore: National Gallery Singapore.

Mahmood, Datin Seri Endon, 2004. *The Nyonya Kebaya – A Century of Straits Chinese Costume.* Singapore: Periplus Editions.

National Gallery Singapore, 2015. *Siapa Nama Kamu? Art in Singapore Since the 19th Century.* Singapore: National Gallery Singapore.

Noor, Farish. A., 2003. *Spirit of Wood – The Art of Malay Woodcarving.* Singapore: Periplus Editions.

Pandeya, Avinash, C., 1943. *The Art of Kathakali.* Allahabad: Kitabistan.

Regina Kraal, John Guy (Ed), Julian Raby (Ed.) and J. Keith Wilson (Ed.), 2011. *Shipwrecked – Tang Treasures and Monsoon Winds.* USA: Smithsonian Books.

Rooney, Dawn F., 1993. *Betel Chewing Traditions in Southeast Asia.* Kuala Lumpur: Oxford University Press.

Sharp, Ilsa, 1993. *The Singapore Cricket Club, Established 1852.* Singapore: Singapore Cricket Club.

Smend, Rudolf and Harper, Donald, 2016. *Batik – Traditional Textiles of Indonesia. From the Rudolf Smend and Donald Harper Collections.* Singapore: Tuttle Publishing.

Soneji, Davesh, 2012. *Bharatanatyam – A Reader.* India: Oxford India Paperbacks.

Tan, Bonny, 2017. "Singapore Cricket Club." *Singapore Infopedia.* Singapore: National Library Board. Available at: http://eresources.nlb.gov.sg/infopedia/articles/SIP_144_2004-12-30.html.

Tan, Bonny and Creamer, Ruth, 2016. "Liu Kang." *Singapore Infopedia.* Singapore: National Library Board. Available at: http://eresources.nlb.gov.sg/infopedia/articles/SIP_158_2005-01-22.html?s=nanyang%20style.

Tan, Kaylene, 2014. "Chen Chong Swee." *Singapore Infopedia.* Singapore: National Library Board. Available at: http://eresources.nlb.gov.sg/infopedia/articles/SIP_2014-01-23_105013.html?s=nanyang%20style.

Tan, Kevin Y. L., 2015. *Of Whales and Dinosaurs – The Story of Singapore's Natural History Museum.* Singapore: NUS Press.

Vasu, Suchittra, 2017. "Lion dance." *Singapore Infopedia*. Singapore: National Library Board. Available at: http://eresources.nlb.gov.sg/infopedia/articles/SIP_57_2004-12-27.html?s=lion%20dance.

Vasu, Suchittra, 2017. "Betel Chewing." *Singapore Infopedia*. Singapore: National Library Board. Available at: http://eresources.nlb.gov.sg/infopedia/articles/SIP_883_2004-12-17.html?s=betel.

Venkataraman, Leela, 2015. *Indian Classical Dance – The Renaissance and Beyond*. India: Niyogi Books.

Vente, Ines, 1984. *Wayang – Chinese Street Opera in Singapore*. Singapore: MPH Bookstores.

Yeo, Alicia, 2016. "Cheong Soo Pieng." *Singapore Infopedia*. Singapore: National Library Board. Available at: http://eresources.nlb.gov.sg/infopedia/articles/SIP_1254_2006-11-30.html?s=nanyang%20style.

Yeo, Wei Wei, 2010. *Cheong Soo Pieng – Visions of Southeast Asia*. Singapore: National Gallery Singapore.

Yeo, Wei Wei, 2011. *Liu Kang – Colourful Modernist*. Singapore: National Gallery Singapore.

FLORA & FAUNA

Archer, Mildred, 1992. *Company Paintings – Indian Paintings for the British Period*. London: Victoria and Albert Museum.

Arunasalam, Sitragandi, Ong, Eng Chuan and Lim, Fiona, 2017. "Vanda Miss Joaquim." *Singapore Infopedia*. Singapore: National Library Board. Available at: http://eresources.nlb.gov.sg/infopedia/articles/SIP_752_2005-01-10.html?s=vanda.

Badenhuizen, Nicolaas, 1995. "The Botanical Garden at Bogor, Java". *In Canadian Journal of Netherlandic Studies*. Issue XVI, Vol ii, Fall 1995, pgs 1 - 4. Toronto: University of Toronto.

Baker, Nick and Lim, Kelvin, 2008. *Wild Animals of Singapore – A Photographic Guide to Mammals, Reptiles, Amphibians and Freshwater Fishes*. Singapore: University of Hawaii Press.

Barnard, Timothy P., 2016. *Nature's Colony: Empire, Nation and Environment in the Singapore Botanic Gardens*. Singapore: N US Press.

Bastin, John S. et al., 2010. *Natural History Drawings: The Complete William Farquhar collection: Malay Peninsula, 1803–1818*. Singapore: Editions Didier Millet and National Museum of Singapore.

Choo-Toh, Get Ten et al, 1985. *A Guide to the Bukit Timah Nature Reserve*. Singapore: Singapore Science Centre.

Davis, Ada and Taylor, Nigel, 2015. *A Walk Through History – A Guide to the Singapore Botanic Gardens*. Singapore: National Parks Board.

Dussek, Ormonde Theodore, 1915. *Hikayat pelandok: Ia-itu hikayat sang kanchil, cherita pelandok dengan anak memerang, hikayat pelandok jenaka*. Singapore: Methodist Publishing House.

Hails, Christopher and Jarvis, Frank, 1990. *Birds of Singapore*. Singapore: Times Editions.

Hew, Choy Sin., Yam, Tim Wing and Arditti, Joseph, 2002. *Biology of Vanda Ms Joaquim*. Singapore: NUS Press.

Johnson, Harold and Wright, Nadia, 2008. *Vanda Miss Joaquim: Singapore's National Flower and The Legacy Of Agnes And Ridley*. Singapore: Suntree Media.

Keay, John, 2006. *The Spice Route – A History*. Berkeley: University of California Press.

Kipling, Rudyard, 1894. *The Jungle Book*. New York: Century & Co. E-book available at: http://www.gutenberg.org/ebooks/35997.

Lee, Meiyu and Lim, Fiona, 2015. "Bukit Timah Nature Reserve." *Singapore Infopedia*. Singapore: National

Library Board. Available at: http://eresources.nlb.gov.sg/infopedia/articles/SIP_55_2004-12-20.html?s=bukit%20timah.

Lim, Charlotte, and Tan, Alicia Yen Ping (Illustration), 2013. *Attack of the Swordfish and Other Singaporean Tales*. Singapore: National Heritage Board.

Ling, Judy, 2009. *Bukit Timah Nature Reserve*. Australia: MacMillan Education Australia.

Lum, Shawn and Sharp, Ilsa, 1996. *A View from the Summit – The Story of Bukit Timah Nature Reserve*. Singapore: Nanyang Technological University and National University of Singapore.

Magee, Judith, 2013. *The Art of India. (Images of Nature)*. London: Natural History Museum.

Magee, Judith, 2013. *Chinese Art and the Reeves Collection. (Images of Nature)*. London: Natural History Museum.

Mukunthan, Michael and Patkar, Akshata, 2017. "Agnes Joaquim." *Singapore Infopedia*. Singapore: National Library Board. Available at: http://eresources.nlb.gov.sg/infopedia/articles/SIP_838_2004-12-24.html?s=vanda.

Nabhan, Gary Paul, 2014. *Cumin, Caramels, and Caravans – A Spice Odyssey*. Berkeley: University of California Press.

National Library Board, 2016. "Henry Nicholas Ridley." *Singapore Infopedia*. Singapore: National Library Board. Available at: http://eresources.nlb.gov.sg/infopedia/articles/SIP_518_2004-12-28.html.

Ng, Peter K. L., Corlett, Richard T. and Tan, Hugh T. W., 2011. *Singapore Biodiversity – An Encyclopedia of the Natural Environment and Sustainable Development*. Singapore: Editions Didiers-Millet.

Noltie, Henry J., 2009. *Raffles' Ark Redrawn – Natural History Drawings from the Collection of Sir Thomas Stamford Raffles*. London: Natural History Museum.

Ong, Christopher, 2009. "Nathaniel Wallich." *Singapore Infopedia*. Singapore: National Library Board. Available at: http://eresources.nlb.gov.sg/infopedia/articles/SIP_1454_2009-02-10.html.

Pires, Tomé, 1515. *The Suma Oriental – an Account of the East, from the Red Sea to Japan, written in Malacca and India in 1512 – 1515. 1944 Edition.* London: Printed for the Hakluyt Society. E-book available at: https://archive.org/details/McGillLibrary-136385-182.

Polunin, Ivan, 1991. *Plants and Flowers of Singapore*. Singapore: Times Editions.

Pwee, Timothy, 2016. "Mousedeer." *Singapore Infopedia*. Singapore: National Library Board. Available at: http://eresources.nlb.gov.sg/infopedia/articles/SIP_1527_2009-05-21.html?s=mousedeer.

Rosengarten Jr, Frederic, 1969. *The Book of Spices*. New York: Pyramid Books.

Skeat, Walter William, 1900. *Malay Magic – being An Introduction to the Folklore and Popular Religion of the Malay Peninsula.* London: MacMillan and Co, Ltd. E-book available at: https://archive.org/details/malaymagicbeingi00skeauoft.

Sim, William, 2017. Botanical Singapore: An Illustrated Guide to Popular Plants and Flowers. Singapore: Marshall Cavendish International.

Tan, Peter W. C., Tan, Aileen and Lau, Laure, 2014. *Singapore Rubber Trade – An Economic Heritage*. Singapore: Suntree Media.

Tinsley, Bonnie, 1983. *Singapore Green – A History and Guide to the Botanic Gardens*. Singapore: Times Books International.

Tinsley, Bonnie, 2009. *Gardens of Perpetual Summer – The Singapore Botanic Gardens*. Singapore: Times Books International.

Wallace, Alfred, 1890. *The Malay Archipelago: The Land of the Orang-utan and the Bird of Paradise – A Narrative of Travel with Studies of Man and Nature.* London: MacMillan and Co. E-book available at: http://wallace-online.org/converted/pdf/1890_MalayArchipelago_S715[10th].pdf.

Wee, Yeow Chin, 1992. *A Guide to the Bukit Timah Nature Reserve*. Singapore: Nature Society and Mobile Oil Singapore.

Welch, Stuart Cary, 1978. *Room for Wonder: Indian Court Painting during the British Period, 1760–1880*. Exhibition catalogue. New York: American Federation of Arts.

Wong Wilson, 2017. *Singapore Chronicles: FLORA AND FAUNA*. Singapore: Institute of Policy Studies and Straits Times Press.

Wright, Nadia, Locke, Linda and Johnson, Harold, 2018. "Blooming Lies – The Vanda Miss Joaquim Story." In *Biblioasia* Volume 14 Issue 01, April – June 2018. Singapore: National Library Board.

Yong, Ding Li and Lim, Kim Chuah, 2016. *A Naturalist's Guide to the Birds of Singapore*. Singapore: John Beaufoy Publishing.

Zaccheus, Melody, 2016. "Vanda Miss Joaquim's namesake get official credit." In *The Straits Times*. 7 September 2016. Singapore: The Straits Times.

Zahari, Rahimiddin, 2015. *Sang Kancil and the Crocodiles*. Translated by Linda Tan and Peter Duke. Kuala Lumpur: Institut Terjemahan & Buku Malaysia Berhad.

Zahari, Rahimuddin, 2015. *Sang Kancil and the Tiger*. Kuala Lumpur: Institut Terjemahan & Buku Malaysia Berhad.

ACKNOWLEDGMENTS

The seed for this book was planted in the course of writing an earlier book on the history of heritage preservation, for which the author had had the privilege of interviewing many heritage professionals in Singapore. The author wishes to thank all these professionals and many more who spend their lives and careers championing heritage preservation. The author wishes also to thank colleagues at the Asian Civilisations Museum, the Peranakan Museum, the National Museum of Singapore, the Indian Heritage Centre and the National Heritage Board for their invaluable support and advice. Finally, he wishes to thank Mr Suhaimi bin Nasrain for imparting wisdom on Malay heritage, spirituality and weaponry, in particular, the keris; and to acknowledge Dr Julian Davison for being quite arguably the best authority on historic Singaporean architecture today.

IMAGE CREDITS

All photography, prints, postcards and other archival material are the author's except where listed below.

The author and publisher would like to thank the following individuals, institutions and museums for their contribution towards the telling of this story of Singapore's heritage. Every possible effort has been made to identify, locate and contact owners of copyright and to seek formal permission for reproducing these images.

Courtesy of Antiques of the Orient. Pages 14 (bottom left), 85, 113 (bottom), 115, 131.

Collection of Asian Civilisations Museum and Peranakan Museum, National Heritage Board. Pages 8, 104 (left and top right), 104 (bottom right) – Gift of Professor Cheah Jin Seng, 116 (top left) – Gift of Iqbal and Maniza Jumabhoy, 116 (top right and bottom left), 116 (bottom right) – Acquired with funds from the Kwan Im Thong Hood Cho Temple, 129, 130 (bottom), 136, 140 (top left, right top and right bottom), 144, 145 – Gift of Digna Cruzem, 146 (left, top and bottom), 150 (all).

Collection of Asian Civilisations Museum and Peranakan Museum, National Heritage Board. Gift of Mr and Mrs Lee Kip Lee. Pages 102, 140 (bottom), 148 (left and right).

Courtesy of Mr KP Bhaskar and Mrs Santha Bhaskar. Collection of Indian Heritage Centre Resource Library. Page 127 (left).

Collection of the British Library. Page 28 (bottom).

Courtesy of Julian Davison. Page 74 (all).

Courtesy of Mr Hsien Yoong How. Page 44 (bottom).

Courtesy of Mrs Rati Kartigesu. Collection of Indian Heritage Centre Resource Library. Page 127 (right).

Courtesy of John Koh. Page 67.

Courtesy of Jacker Lau. Page 177.

Courtesy of Mr and Mrs Lee Kip Lee. Pages 93 (centre), 110.

Courtesy of Lim Kheng Chye. Pages 42, 56, 65, 66 (bottom), 107 (bottom), 123, 133.

Courtesy of Linda Locke. Page 167.

Courtesy of Emily Marcar and the late Arshak Galstaun, via Ilsa Sharp, Perth, Western Australia (author, 'There Is Only One Raffles', Souvenir Press, London 1981/1986 – Souvenir Press Ltd, London, 1st Edition ISBN 0 285 62383 4, and 2nd Edition ISBM: 0 285 62744 9). Page 114.

Collection of National Gallery Singapore. Courtesy of National Heritage Board. Page 152 (top) – Gift of the artist, 152 (bottom left) – Gift of DBS Bank Ltd.

Collection of National Gallery Singapore. Courtesy of National Gallery Singapore. Page 152 (bottom right) – Gift of Lee Foundation.

Collection of the National Portrait Gallery, London. Page 18.

Collection of National Museum of Singapore, National Heritage Board. Pages 10, 17, 20, 21, 22, 23, 24, 30, 33, 40 – Gift of Dr John Hall Jones, 45, 47 – Gift of PSA, 55, 58, 63, 72, 73, 80, 83 (top), 85, 87, 89 (top), 93 (left and right), 94 (left and right), 95, 97 (left and right), 101 – Gift of LTC Lim Eng Lian, 104 (centre), 105, 106 (bottom left and bottom right), 111 (top and bottom), 112 (left) – Gift of the Armenian Church, 112 (right), 113 (top), 117, 120, 122 (top), 130 (top), 138, 142, 143, 146 (top), 156, 164, 171, 173.

Collection of National Museum of Singapore, National Heritage Board. Gift of Mr. G.K. Goh. Pages 154, 157, 161 (top and bottom), 165, 169.

Collection of Mr John Nicholson. Pages 28 – 29 (top), 36 – 37, 66 (top).

Courtesy of Cedric Pereira. Page 98.

Courtesy of Jeff Tan. Page 175.

Courtesy of Luca Invernizzi Tettoni. Pages 2, 76 (top and bottom), 78 (bottom left and right), 134 (left and right).

Images in the Public Domain. Pages 26, 106.

Images from Creative Commons.
Page 61 (bottom) – By Kok Leng Yeo, "Rodolfo Nolli's sculpture Allegory of Justice on the tympanum of the Old Supreme Court Building, Singapore," licensed under the Creative Commons Attribution 2.0 Generic License. https://commons.wikimedia.org/wiki/File:AllegoryofJustice-Old-SupremeCourtBuilding-Singapore-20071013.jpg.

Page 124 – By Qnonsense, "A Kathakali performer in the virtuous pachcha (green) role at Kochi, India", licensed under the Creative Commons Attribution-Share Alike 3.0 Unported License. https://commons.m.wikimedia.org/wiki/File:Kathakalidancer.jpg.

Page 127 – By Suyash Dwivedi, "Bharatanatyam Facial expressions Mudra (18)", licensed under the Creative Commons Attribution-Share Alike 4.0 International License. https://commons.m.wikimedia.org/wiki/File:Bharatanatyam_Mudra_(18).jpg

INDEX